The Birder's Guide
to Vancouver and the Lower Mainland

The Birder's Guide

to Vancouver and
the Lower Mainland

Edited by Catherine J. Aitchison

Vancouver Natural
History Society

WHITECAP BOOKS
Vancouver/Toronto/New York

Edited by Elaine Jones
Proofread by Naomi Pauls, Paper Trail Publishing
Cover design by Tanya Lloyd/Spotlight Designs
Interior design by Warren Clark
Interior illustrations by Allyson MacBean
Maps by Gary Kaiser and Roland Wahlgren

Printed and bound in Canada

National Library of Canada Cataloguing in Publication Data
    Birder's guide to Vancouver and the Lower Mainland

    Includes bibliographical references and index.
    ISBN 1-55285-207-5

    1. Bird-watching—British Columbia—Vancouver Metropolitan
Area—Guidebooks. 2. Birds—British Columbia—Vancouver
Metropolitan Area. I. Vancouver Natural History Society.
QL685.5.B7B5734 2001   598'.07'23471133   C2001-910530-4

The publisher acknowledges the support of the Canada Council for the
Arts and the Cultural Services Branch of the Government of British
Columbia for our publishing program. We acknowledge the financial
support of the Government of Canada through the Book Publishing
Industry Development Program for our publishing activities.

Cover photographs: Steller's Jay by Roy Hamaguchi;
Rufous Hummingbird and Flowering Currant by Edwin G.A. Willcox;
Saw-whet Owl by Virginia Hayes; Bald Eagle by Edwin G.A. Willcox

Contents

Foreword

I am sitting in a sidewalk cafe on West Broadway on a sunny August morning. House Sparrows chatter from the trees across the street and the occasional pigeon flies over, but at last my birding eyes are truly rewarded as a beautiful Bald Eagle soars in the blue sky. Vancouver is a special place for birds and birdwatchers. Nestled between towering mountains and the rich waters of the Pacific, it offers an interface between wilderness and urban environments like few other cities on earth.

This interface provides fabulous birding opportunities, from the muddy Fraser River delta and its shorebirds to songbirds in the high mountain meadows of Cypress Bowl and the rafts of winter water-fowl on English Bay. It is perhaps best illustrated by Stanley Park, a mix of ancient forest and seashore within easy walking distance of the urban core of Vancouver.

I enjoyed birding in the Vancouver area for 25 years as a local resident, and now visit several times a year, binoculars always close at hand. I still revel at the sight of Band-tailed Pigeons rocketing through the autumn sky, busy flocks of Bushtits lisping through salmonberry thickets and clouds of Black Swifts wheeling in the June rain. As the city changes, I'll need a birding guide like this more and more, and I'm sure that Vancouver residents and visitors alike will find it an invaluable help in maximizing their birding pleasure in this special part of the world.

Dick Cannings

Acknowledgements

The efforts of many people have gone into the preparation of this book, which is a totally revised version of a book published by the Vancouver Natural History Society in 1993, *A Birdwatching Guide to the Vancouver Area British Columbia*. The information in that book has been thoroughly revised, updated and rewritten, and information on several new areas has been added. All the maps are completely new, and the section of colour photographs allows several members to showcase their fine work. Three new sidebars, "Crested Mynas," "Tides" and "Bears and Other Wild Animals," have been included to make this new book as comprehensive as possible for birders.

Many members of the VNHS contributed their time and expertise to this project. The names of the authors and revisors may be found at the end of each section, however, the following is a complete list: Catherine J. Aitchison, Patricia M. Banning-Lover, Kevin Bell, Dick Cannings, George Clulow, Larry Cowan, Adrian Grant Duff, Kyle Elliott, Carlo Giovanella, Al Grass, Eric Greenwood, John Ireland, Dale Jensen, Ken Klimko, Hue and Jo Ann MacKenzie, Martin K. McNicholl, Bill Merilees, Brian Scott, Brian Self, Daphne Solecki, Richard Swanston, Rick Toochin, Danny Tyson and Jack Williams. The authors of several of the original chapters were not able to participate this time because of constraints of time or distance. Their work formed the basis of some of the sections that have been revised by others. They are: Gerry Ansell, John and Shirley Dorsey, Sue-Ellen Fast, Christine Hanrahan, Brian Kautesk, Robin Owen, Mary Peet-Leslie, Thomas Plath, Allen Poynter, Michael Price, Val Schaefer and Wayne Weber.

Catherine J. Aitchison was responsible for compiling the material submitted, editing the text and photographs, doing the word processing and co-ordinating the project. Martin K. McNicholl contributed many hours of proofreading and provided a great deal of assistance and advice on content and technical details. Larry Cowan, Jude Grass, Daphne Solecki, Rex Kenner and Al Maki also proofread various portions of the book. The Burns Bog section was read by Eliza Olsen and Sarah Howie of the Burns Bog Conservation Society, who provided valuable information about the bog and the issues involved there. Elaine Jones and Robin Rivers of Whitecap Books gave valuable editing and production advice.

The new maps were jointly produced by Gary Kaiser and Roland Wahlgren. The bar-graph checklist was produced for the Vancouver Natural History Society by Rick Toochin, with computer design and data entry by Tom Brown and Kyle Elliott. The "Selected List of Vancouver Bird Species" was written originally by Wayne Weber and has been revised and updated by Danny Tyson, with input from Kyle Elliott.

Photographers whose work enlivens this book are: Carol Fuegi, Al and Jude Grass, Roy Hamaguchi, Virginia Hayes, Lothar Kirchner, Bill Merilees, Allen Poynter, Osborne Shaw and Edwin G.A. Willcox. Patricia M. Banning-Lover kindly provided access to the Wild Bird Trust photo collection, and John Ireland did the same for the Reifel Migratory Bird Sanctuary photo collection. The line drawings of birds were done by Allyson MacBean.

Eric Greenwood applied his computer expertise to several thorny problems. Daphne Solecki and George Bangham also lent their computers and time to the project. Formatting of the first draft was done by Cathy Brannen, and the second draft was formatted and checked by Pam Dicer. Daphne Solecki, Jeremy McCall and Cathy Brannen handled the contract for the book.

Many thanks to Daphne Solecki for her continuing support and advice throughout the production of this book, and also to Jeremy McCall and the VNHS Board of Directors.

Introduction

The Vancouver area is one of the most spectacular places in which to observe birds in North America. It contains a vast array of habitat types—mountains, forests, bogs, freshwater lakes and streams, marine inlets and bays, freshwater lakes and brackish marshes, mud flats and rocky shorelines. Over 260 species of birds can be seen here on an annual basis, and over 400 species have been seen more than once.

In addition to providing birding opportunities through a diversity of habitat types, the Fraser River estuary is also a major staging point on the Pacific Flyway. Millions of shorebirds and waterfowl pass through here on their migratory routes between Siberia, Alaska and northern Canada, and California, Central America and South America. The region is also an important wintering area for raptors.

The Ecology of Greater Vancouver

Greater Vancouver's natural environment encompasses four large systems.

- Along the mountainous North Shore is a large forest association of western hemlock, western redcedar and Douglas-fir, which extends for 50 km (31 mi) between the Strait of Georgia and Pitt Lake. This area is full of ravines and canyons, and there are three large freshwater lakes (Capilano, Seymour and Coquitlam) that provide Vancouver-area residents with their drinking water.
- Along the shoreline is the coastal/intertidal area, rich in marine life. Brackish marshes are found at Roberts Bank and Sturgeon Bank to the west of the cities of Delta and Richmond. Mud flats are found at Boundary Bay and Semiahmoo Bay to the south, and at Maplewood and Port Moody in Burrard Inlet to the north. Rocky shorelines occur along most of Burrard Inlet and Indian Arm.

- The major freshwater environment is represented by the Fraser River system. As it passes through Greater Vancouver the Fraser River divides into three arms. The South Arm is the largest of the three and carries 80 percent of the water flow. Other major freshwater bodies associated with the Fraser River are the Brunette River system (which includes Burnaby and Deer lakes) in Burnaby and New Westminster; Pitt Lake and the Pitt River in Port Coquitlam and Pitt Meadows; the Coquitlam River in Coquitlam; and the Salmon River, which runs through Coquitlam, Langley, Fort Langley and Surrey.
- The Fraser Lowland System includes numerous creeks and the (Little) Campbell, Serpentine and Nicomekl rivers with their flood plains in Surrey and Delta. Along with the Fraser River, they all form the Fraser River delta, which covers 590 square km (228 square mi), the largest of the deltas on Canada's Pacific coast. Burns Bog in Delta and Sea and Iona islands in Richmond form part of this system.

Birdlife in the Vancouver area is changing because of rapid human population growth. More than half the population of British Columbia, about 2 million people, is concentrated in the lower Fraser River basin, and urban sprawl has resulted in considerable loss of habitat. The dyking of wetlands is a major concern. Seventy percent of the original freshwater marshes and 90 percent of the saltwater and brackish marshes have been lost over the last 100 years.

The introduction and expansion of range of alien bird species has also had an impact on local bird species. European Starlings first appeared in B.C. about 50 years ago. Flocks of thousands of these birds are now common around Vancouver. Starlings displace many local hole-nesting species such as Purple Martins. The decline of Crested Mynas, another alien species, is thought to be directly related to competition for nest-holes from starlings. Other invasive species that have had a negative impact on bird populations are eastern gray squirrels and Virginia opossums.

Many parks and sanctuaries have been created in an effort to preserve and encourage birdlife. The Greater Vancouver Regional District Parks system contains 10,000 ha (24,700 a) of valuable bird habitat. There are many municipal parks as well, including the famous Stanley Park in Vancouver's West End. Wildlife refuges include Reifel Migratory Bird Sanctuary in Ladner and Pitt-Addington Marsh in Pitt Meadows.

Its diverse habitats and its important role as a migratory stopover and wintering area for many species make the Vancouver area an exciting place to watch birds in all seasons of the year. The Vancouver Christmas Bird Count consistently places in the top three counts in Canada in terms of number of species seen—usually between 145 and 150 species. There are unique species, such as Crested Mynas, and unique concentrations of other species, such as shorebirds, waterfowl and raptors. Up to 60 percent of the world population of Barrow's Goldeneyes winters in the Vancouver area.

How to Use This Book

The sites described here are grouped by general location in the Vancouver area. A wide range of habitats is represented. These are some of the favourite spots of members of the Vancouver Natural History Society (VNHS). Of course, there are many other areas, too numerous to document in this book, which are very well worth birding. Information on specific sites not mentioned here can be obtained by contacting one of the volunteers who maintain the VNHS Vancouver Bird Alert line (see page 14).

Each section contains directions for getting to the site by car from downtown Vancouver. Information on public transit routes is included where it is available. A site map is provided for ease in locating key roads, paths and other features. Residents and long-term visitors will find the annually updated, detailed map books of Greater Vancouver helpful, especially in locating obscure sites listed on the Bird Alert. These are available at many gas stations, drug-stores and convenience stores throughout Greater Vancouver.

Descriptions for each location contain an overview of the major species to be found there, especially those birds that are most likely

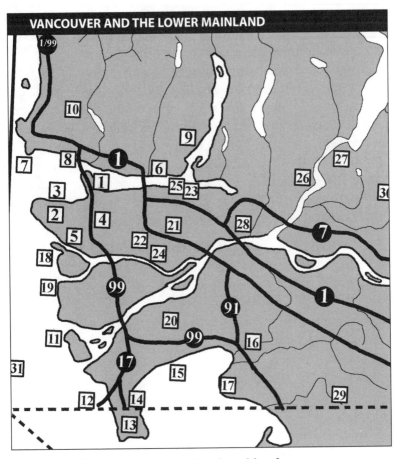

VANCOUVER AND THE LOWER MAINLAND

Numbers refer to locations listed in the table of contents.

Legend for maps

 Walking path

Marsh

 Highway

to be found, as well as an indication of the possibility of unusual numbers or species. This will enable birders to prepare field identification skills for certain species before visiting a site.

The Vancouver Natural History Society conducts about 150 field trips of various types annually, and visitors are welcome to attend as an introduction to nature in the Vancouver area. Information about upcoming trips, membership and special events is available on the VNHS Events and Information line at (604) 737-3074. This number also contains the Vancouver Bird Alert, which is updated as necessary, usually every day or two. See "Helpful Information," page 224, for more information on the VNHS and other local and provincial organizations.

Written by Val Schaefer; revised by Catherine J. Aitchison

Vancouver Natural History Society
P.O. Box 3021, Vancouver, B.C. V6B 3X5
Events and Information, and **Bird Alert**
Tel: (604) 737-3074, 24 hours a day

Vancouver

1. Stanley Park

Stanley Park, arguably the most famous urban park in Canada, is a 405-ha (1,000-a) peninsula of beautiful forests, gardens, freshwater lakes and saltwater shorelines, located next to Vancouver's densely populated West End. It was established in 1888, only two years after the City of Vancouver was incorporated. Although the park has a history of disturbance—partial logging in the 1860s, Typhoon Frieda in 1962, numerous blow-downs as a result of windstorms, recreational development and tree removal—it still has some good examples of relatively undisturbed old-growth forest. These stands consist of western redcedar, western hemlock and Douglas-fir. About two-thirds of the roughly 250 ha (617 a) of forest is classified as mature coniferous (over 100 years old). The remainder of the park is given over to gardens and recreational areas, including a pitch-and-putt golf course, the Vancouver Aquarium, beaches, picnic areas and playing fields. An extensive trail system (mostly poorly signposted) winds throughout the park.

The seawall walk is continually expanding and it is now possible to walk from the downtown harbour side all the way around Stanley Park, and on around English Bay and False Creek. Walking (or bicycling) along the seawall may be particularly rewarding in late fall/winter or early spring, as the waters off the seawall are prime habitat for **ducks**, **loons**, **grebes** and **cormorants**. With more than 230 species of birds reliably reported from the park, and new ones added every year, it has been a favourite birding area of Vancouverites for generations.

Directions

Only about 1.5 km (.9 mi) from downtown Vancouver, Stanley Park is easily reached on foot by walking west along any street through the residential area of the West End. Robson Street, Davie Street and Beach Avenue are three of the main east-west streets.

By car, drive west on Georgia Street and take the Stanley Park exit to the right just opposite Lost Lagoon, or head north along English Bay on Beach Avenue. The drive that encircles the park is one-way counter-clockwise. From North or West Vancouver, drive south across the Lions Gate Bridge (Highway 99) and turn right immediately after entering the park. This exit joins the park drive near Prospect Point, but is closed during morning rush hours to discourage commuter traffic. There are numerous parking areas along the drive and pay parking is in effect throughout the park, even on

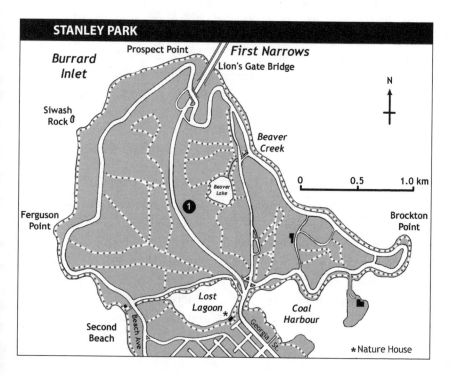

the roadways—make sure you display your receipt on your dashboard.

To reach the park by bus from downtown Vancouver, take the #135 Stanley Park bus on Georgia Street, which stops at the park entrance beside Lost Lagoon. In the summer, there is a bus service around the park with stops at major attractions.

The Stanley Park Nature House, run by the Stanley Park Ecology Society, is located in the old boathouse building at Lost Lagoon, near the corner of Chilco and Alberni streets. This is not obvious from street level. Take the path beside the lagoon or the steps down to water level from the top of the building, which at present forms a small street-level viewing area. Park maps, bird checklists and nature books, as well as information about the park, are available here. The Nature House organizes a waterfowl count on Lost Lagoon at 9 A.M. every Saturday (free of charge) and two-hour Discovery Walks on Sundays at 1 P.M. (for a small charge). The Nature House hours are: April/May and September/October, Friday to Sunday 11 A.M. to 5 P.M.; June to August, 11 A.M. to 7 P.M., closed Tuesdays; November to March, Friday to Sunday 11 A.M. to 3 P.M.

Bird Species

WINTER

Lost Lagoon is perhaps the most familiar birding spot in Stanley Park. From late September to early May, the lagoon teems with water birds. These are mainly *diving ducks*, but there are also hundreds of *Canada Geese*, *Mallards* and *American Coots* and smaller numbers of other species. The commonest diving ducks are *Greater* and *Lesser scaup*, *Common Goldeneyes* and *Barrow's Goldeneyes*. Most of the goldeneyes use the lagoon as a nighttime roost, departing at dawn and returning in late afternoon. The *Lesser Scaup* seem to do the opposite, apparently feeding elsewhere at night and sleeping in the lagoon during the day. Lost Lagoon is an excellent place to learn to distinguish *Greater Scaup* from *Lesser Scaup*. The park's wing-clipped **Mute Swans** are not successful nesters each year, although three cygnets were raised to adulthood in 1999 and two in 2000. However, the swans remain a captive species and are not countable. Over the years, the Mute Swans have occasionally been joined by one or two wild **Trumpeter Swans** for varying periods of time. Thirty or 40 **Canvasbacks** are usually present, and this is one of the few places where wild Canvasbacks can be seen as close as 3 to 4 m (10 to 13 ft). A small marsh was started in 2000 in one corner of Lost Lagoon opposite the Nature House. It remains to be seen what additional species may be attracted to it.

Lost Lagoon is the best place in Vancouver to find **Ring-necked Ducks** or **Redheads**. A Redhead is often present in the lagoon in the winter, and up to ten Ring-necked Ducks have been counted. Occasionally, a very rare duck shows up. The first **Tufted Duck** ever seen in Canada was sighted here in 1961, and one of these rare old-world ducks has been present for part of the winter at least every other year since then.

Do not miss the stone bridge, which crosses the creek at the west end of Lost Lagoon: it is a great spot for winter birding. The tangle of shrubbery next to the bridge contains several feeders that are usually hopping with **Dark-eyed Juncos**, **Song** and **Fox sparrows**, **Spotted Towhees**, **Black-capped Chickadees**, **Red-winged Blackbirds** and an occasional **Golden-crowned Sparrow** or **Brown-headed Cowbird**. The feeders often allow close looks at normally shy forest birds like **Chestnut-backed Chickadees** and **Red-breasted Nuthatches**. Sometimes they will even eat from your hand. Closer inspection of the shrubbery will usually reveal more birds. A **Virginia Rail** wintered here for several seasons and a **Harris's Sparrow** has turned up also. A few **Wood Ducks** can usually be seen in the water near here.

The coniferous forests that cover much of Stanley Park are often very quiet in winter. You may walk for more than a kilometre without seeing a bird, then suddenly find yourself surrounded by a mixed-species feeding flock. These flocks usually include **Golden-crowned** and **Ruby-crowned kinglets**, **Black-capped** and **Chestnut-**

backed chickadees, a **Brown Creeper** or two, and often a **Red-breasted Nuthatch** or a **Downy** or **Hairy woodpecker**. The frantic activity lasts a few moments, and then all is silent again. Along the dank and often dripping trails, you may be lucky enough to spot a **Red-breasted Sapsucker** or a **Pileated Woodpecker**, but there are generally more land birds around the alder stands and ornamental plantings than in the coniferous forest.

In winter, a walk along the Stanley Park seawall allows you to see impressive numbers of diving ducks, especially **Surf Scoters** and **Barrow's Goldeneyes**. Vancouver has the largest known winter concentrations of Barrow's Goldeneyes in the world, as documented by the Vancouver Natural History Society's Christmas Bird Counts. A raft of 4,000 or more **Western Grebes** usually winters in English Bay off Ferguson Point. Other common winter water birds include **Red-throated** and **Common loons**, **Horned** and **Red-necked grebes**, **Double-crested** and **Pelagic cormorants**, **American Wigeon**, **Greater Scaup**, **Long-tailed Ducks**, **Black Scoters**, **Common Goldeneyes**, **Buffleheads**, **Red-breasted Mergansers**, **Glaucous-winged**, **Mew** and **Thayer's gulls** and **Pigeon Guillemots**. Other species are more localized. **Harlequin Ducks** are likely to be sighted on rocky areas of the shoreline from Ferguson Point to Prospect Point, and a **Brandt's Cormorant** might be seen on the shoal markers on the harbour side of the park near Brockton Point. At low tide, **Black Turnstones** and **Sanderling** can often be seen on the rocks near Ferguson Point, sometimes accompanied by a **Rock Sandpiper** or (rarely) a **Surfbird**. Any group of **American Wigeon** is worth checking out for the occasional **Eurasian Wigeon**. During at least four winters a **King Eider** has accompanied the flocks of **Surf Scoters** in English Bay and a **Common Eider** also recently spent a winter in their company.

SPRING

Spring migration extends from late February, when most of the **American Robin** population arrives, to the first week of June, when a few straggling **Western Wood-Pewees**, **Western Tanagers** and

Wilson's Warblers may still be passing through. However, the peak occurs in late April and early May, when the park may be almost choked with birds some days. The commonest species are **White-crowned** and **Golden-crowned sparrows** and **Yellow-rumped** and **Wilson's warblers**, which may exceed 100 in a day. Look for migrating **songbirds** along forest edges and ornamental plantings (for example, the gardens around the Lost Lagoon pitch-and-putt course) and in the willows at the edge of Lost Lagoon. You can also see them in forested areas, especially among stands of flowering broadleaf maple trees near Brockton Point and Third Beach. Broadleaf maple flowers, which reach their peak in late April, offer a ready supply of insects for the hungry warblers.

Other species of land birds that migrate through Stanley Park include **Vaux's Swifts**, **Rufous Hummingbirds**, **Western Wood-Pewees**, **Tree Swallows**, **Ruby-crowned Kinglets**, **Townsend's Solitaires**, **Hermit** and **Varied thrushes**, **American Pipits**, **Cassin's** and **Warbling vireos**, **Orange-crowned**, **Nashville**, **Yellow**, **Black-throated Gray** and **Townsend's warblers**, **Western Tanagers** and **Savannah** and **Lincoln's sparrows**. Some of these species breed in the park, and most of them are found in both spring and fall, but a few, such as **Townsend's Solitaires** and **Nashville Warblers**, are seen almost exclusively in spring.

Water bird migration in Stanley Park is not as spectacular as it is on the Fraser delta, but you are more likely to see rare or unusual species like a **Yellow-billed Loon**, **Eurasian Wigeon** and **Tufted Duck**. These are more likely seen in early spring than in midwinter.

SUMMER

Some species, such as **Bald Eagles**, begin breeding as early as late February, but most breeding activity takes place from late May through July. The nesting seabird colony on the Prospect Point cliffs, just west of the Lions Gate Bridge, includes 40 to 50 pairs of **Pelagic Cormorants** and a dozen or so pairs of **Glaucous-winged Gulls** and **Pigeon Guillemots**. A few pairs of gulls usually nest on the concrete bases of the bridge towers, and a few gulls and cormorants try to nest on Siwash Rock. You can see the colony best from the seawall walk at its base. A few **Pelagic Cormorants** use this area as a roost throughout the year.

Nesting species in Stanley Park include a pair of **Bald Eagles**, which has in recent years nested near Beaver Lake. Also, a pair of **Common Ravens** is suspected to nest somewhere in the park. However, the dominant breeding species are **Canada Geese**, **Wood Ducks** (which use nest boxes near Beaver Lake) and **Mallards**. In addition to the nesting geese, as many as 1,500 non-breeding or post-breeding geese find safety in the park from late June to early July during their brief flightless period, when they moult their wing feathers.

In June and July, the Beaver Lake area is the best part of the park to see a large variety of birds, partly because its denser forest supports species such as **Hammond's Flycatchers** and **Townsend's Warblers**. You may also find **Hairy Woodpeckers**, **Olive-sided** and **Pacific-slope flycatchers**, **Red-breasted Nuthatches**, **Brown Creepers**, **Golden-crowned Kinglets**, **Cassin's Vireos**, **Orange-crowned**, **Black-throated Gray** and **Wilson's warblers**, **Western Tanagers** and **Black-headed Grosbeaks**. In the shrubbery around the lake look for breeding **Willow Flycatchers**, **Yellow Warblers**, **Song Sparrows** and **Red-winged Blackbirds**. The lily-choked lake itself has breeding **Wood Ducks**, **Mallards** and, in some years, **Pied-billed Grebes**.

FALL

The fall migration of **land birds** takes place mainly between mid-August and mid-October. Concentrations tend to be smaller than those in spring, in part because of the more stable fall weather. Most of the common land-bird species in fall are the same as those listed for spring, but you have a better chance of seeing an out-of-range vagrant, perhaps because of the high percentage of inexperienced juvenile birds.

During August, migrating shorebirds begin to appear. Repeated visits to Ferguson Point and upper Coal Harbour at low tide, preferably before 10 A.M., may allow you to see **Greater** and **Lesser yellowlegs**, **Least** and **Western sandpipers** and possibly **Black-bellied Plovers** or a **phalarope**.

The most interesting time to go birding is on a cold, clear day with brisk northwest winds following several overcast rainy days. Such weather triggers southward movements of many species, from ducks and birds of prey to sparrows. Northwest winds are especially favourable for observing southward-flying raptors. There is a fall migration route along the North Shore mountains, and some of these birds cross over into Vancouver via Stanley Park. Among the commoner species, like **Red-tailed**, **Sharp-shinned** and **Cooper's hawks**, you may be lucky enough to spot a **Turkey Vulture** or an **Osprey**. On a cold-front day in late September you may also find large numbers of **Yellow-rumped Warblers**, **American Pipits**, **Savannah Sparrows**, **Dark-eyed Juncos** and **Ruby-crowned Kinglets**, as well as late-departing individuals of several other warbler species. After a cold front in mid-October, you may find dozens of **Buffleheads**, a **Ring-necked Duck** or a small flock of **Hooded Mergansers** where there were none the day before.

Along English Bay and Burrard Inlet, look for unusual gulls and terns. Large flocks of **Bonaparte's Gulls** feed offshore from August through December. They are often joined from August through late October by **Common Terns**, which, unlike the Bonaparte's Gulls, are not seen in spring. Small numbers of **Franklin's Gulls** are seen regularly with the Bonaparte's Gulls, and rare species like **Heermann's** and **Sabine's gulls** and **Caspian**, **Arctic** and **Forster's terns** have been recorded. In September and October, **Parasitic Jaegers** are seen regularly off Siwash Rock and Ferguson Point, harassing gulls and terns in an effort to steal fish from them. A scan of English Bay might reveal a **Pigeon Guillemot**, **Marbled Murrelet** or the even more rare **Rhinoceros Auklet**.

Written by Wayne Weber and Brian Kautesk;
revised by Catherine J. Aitchison

2. Pacific Spirit Regional Park

Most of this Greater Vancouver Regional District park is forest, including some of the oldest and most diverse second-growth stands in the Lower Mainland. The forest spreads across a gently rounded, undulating plateau bounded by steep cliffs and gullies with beaches and marsh below. In the early 1860s, the tip of the Point Grey Peninsula was reserved from settlement to defend the Crown Colony from potential American or Russian invaders. The first timber leases were granted in 1865; the entire park has since been logged, much of it selectively. In 1923 the area became an endowment to the future University of British Columbia and several subdivisions were carved out of the forest. Some later subdivision attempts were halted after the land was cleared. The vegetation has since grown back into thick red alder and cottonwood stands. As the city surrounded the remaining woods, the forest became more popular for naturalists, horseback riders and walkers. Today the area is protected within Pacific Spirit Regional Park and contains many different vegetation associations, from abandoned pastureland to mature evergreen forest, beaches and bogs. The diversity of habitats supports numerous bird species.

Directions

Pacific Spirit Regional Park stretches across the tip of the Point Grey Peninsula, just north of the mouth of the Fraser River and west of Vancouver's downtown core. Formerly known as the University Endowment Lands, the park surrounds the University of British Columbia. Over 50 km (31 mi) of trails lead through a mosaic of good birding habitats within minutes of downtown Vancouver. It is easy to reach by car along 4th Avenue, 10th Avenue, 16th Avenue or SW Marine Drive.

From downtown Vancouver, several buses run to the area, but

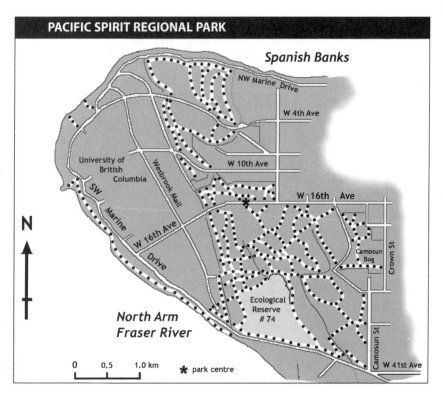

they service the UBC campus, rather than the park itself. Because of
the size of the park, you should consult a good map to determine
the area you want to reach, and choose a bus route accordingly. The
#4 UBC or #10 UBC buses southbound on Granville Street go to the
UBC bus loop on the campus. From there, transfer to a #25
Brentwood bus, which will take you out of the campus and past the
Pacific Spirit Park Centre on 16th Avenue (see below). Ask the bus
driver for the nearest stop. Alternatively, take the #8 Granville bus,
southbound on Granville Street, to King Edward (25th Avenue) and
transfer to the #25 UBC, or to 41st Avenue and transfer to a #41
UBC bus.

The Pacific Spirit Park Centre is located at 4915 West 16th
Avenue on the north side of the road, .5 km (.3 mi) west of Blanca
Street. Maps of the many trails may be obtained here, and there are
washrooms, telephones and drinking water.

Bird Species

Along Marine Drive, all the way around the point, from Spanish Banks past the campus and east again to Camosun Street, look for **Bald Eagles** perched on cedar snags. Several other roads cut through the park, and many more trailheads await exploration at the ends of neighbourhood streets. Start your hike at the Pacific Spirit Park Centre or any one of several trails where they cross major roads.

CONIFEROUS FOREST

The famous west coast evergreens flourish in the large area south of 16th Avenue, where the dense canopy dominated by Douglas-fir rustles with birdlife. You may get tired from peering up into the dark branches, but patience could pay off with good observations of **Brown Creepers**, **Golden-crowned Kinglets** and other, often unseen, species going about their business oblivious of your presence. The movements of hunting **owls** may also catch your eye as they search the open forest floor in the deep shade. **Northern Sawwhet**, **Barred**, **Western Screech** and **Great Horned owls** are known to nest in the park, and others have been sighted. The power line along Imperial Trail cuts a welcome swath through the canopy, and the sunlit salmonberry layer beneath the lines is often busy with birdlife.

Salmonberry begins to bloom in early April some years. As soon as the large magenta blossoms appear, you may hear the zing of foraging male **Rufous Hummingbirds**. Later, as the air warms and the females arrive, watch for their bright courtship flights against the evergreen backdrop. This power line and others in the park are also good places to spot hunting **owls** at dusk, particularly in early fall. South of Imperial Trail, farther from the spine of the peninsula, more moisture in the soil encourages growth of western hemlock, western redcedar and Sitka spruce, resulting in a more diverse rain forest with a thicker deciduous understory. **Purple Finches**, **Winter Wrens** and **Pacific-slope Flycatchers** (in summer) abound. Where large trees have fallen, listen for the song of **Black-throated Gray Warblers** in spring. In the more mixed areas of the forest **Hutton's Vireos** call in the clearings.

DECIDUOUS FOREST

North of 16th Avenue, patches of coniferous and mixed forest can be found, but most of the area has been recently disturbed. Sunny patches of bitter cherry and fragrant black cottonwood interrupt large stands of red alder, while the ravines and steep slopes at the northern edge are full of broadleaf maples. Edges of subdivisions, ravines and clearings provide the best birding spots. The old pasture clearing called the Plains of Abraham at the north end of Pioneer Trail is a sun trap on spring mornings and provides a berry feast in the fall; it is often busy with many species of **songbirds**. Start from the trailhead kiosk on NW Marine Drive just west of the most western concession stand at Spanish Banks, where washrooms and parking are available.

OCEAN BEACH

The rocky beaches west of sandy Spanish Banks are one of the best places in the Vancouver area to view **sea ducks**. All three **scoter species** can be seen here from October to April, as well as **Barrow's Goldeneyes** and other divers. Watch for **shorebirds** too, including **Black Oystercatchers**. Be sure to walk as far as the old searchlight towers, and check the breakwater at Wreck Beach for accidental species blown in from the sea. The city can seem very far away from this wild landscape of wind, waves and towering cliffs. Start from the Acadia trailhead at the park entrance sign on NW Marine Drive, where washrooms and parking are available, or hike down one of the steep trails to Wreck Beach from the campus. Be forewarned that Wreck Beach has clothing-optional status, and sunbathers in a natural state can be encountered on any mild or sunny day.

BOOMING GROUND MARSH

The Wreck Beach breakwater protects the estuarine marsh to the south. Here freshwater from the Fraser River's North Arm collects and logs are stored. The trail follows the base of the steep slope past secluded sunbathing areas. **Marsh Wrens** and other marsh species rustle among the cattails, and **Virginia Rails** have been spotted near the mouth of Booming Grounds Creek close to the park boundary. Various **duck** and **shorebird species** can also be found in this increasingly rare habitat. Walk south from the busy beach area, or hike down from the historic monument parking lot on Marine Drive to the quieter marsh area below.

Written by Sue-Ellen Fast; revised by Adrian Grant Duff

3. Jericho Beach Park

Situated on English Bay, Jericho is probably one of the best city parks for birding found anywhere. At 54 ha (133 a), the park is less than one-sixth the size of Stanley Park, yet can offer almost the same number of species. Many unusual and accidental species have been found here.

The park has had a checkered history and has been much affected by human activity. The name derives from Jerry's Cove, after Jeremiah Rogers, who, in the 1860s, established a base camp on the edge of the wilderness and set about felling the enormous trees that once grew here. A few stumps from this era can be found in the park. Later, picnickers came by barge from downtown Vancouver. The area then became part of a golf course for the Jericho Country Club.

In 1942, the federal Department of National Defence bought most of the land and built an airstrip, remains of which are seen in the large concrete wharf east of the sailing centre. In 1973, the land was sold back to the city to form the park as we see it today.

Birding is good year round, dropping off only in the summer months. Within the park's boundaries are woodland, meadow, freshwater marsh and ponds, scrub, flat grassy areas, sandy foreshore and a saltwater bay. The best time to visit is early morning.

Directions

Jericho Beach Park is located on the north side of West 4th Avenue, between Wallace and Discovery streets. It is served by the #4 Fourth and #42 Spanish Banks buses, and is only a short walk from the #7 Dunbar stop at West 4th Avenue and Alma Street. The park can be entered anywhere along its perimeter and cycling is permitted. No cars are allowed; however, there is ample parking along West 4th Avenue and in pay parking lots (free in winter months).

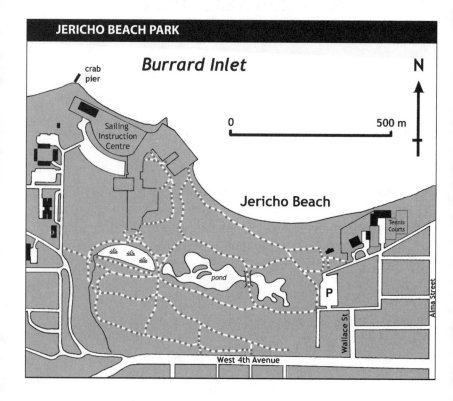

From Jericho Beach, depending on tides, you can walk west along Spanish Banks to the Point Grey headland or east along rocky Bayswater Beach to Kitsilano Beach.

Bird Species

From October through May, this is an excellent location for waterfowl. Between the freshwater ponds and the bay, almost every common local species may be found, including **Wood Ducks**, a few **Eurasian Wigeon** among the flocks of **American Wigeon**, **Green-winged Teal**, **Greater** and **Lesser scaup**, **Common** and **Barrow's goldeneyes**, **Surf**, **White-winged** and **Black scoters**, **Common** and **Red-breasted mergansers** and **Long-tailed Ducks**. On the saltwater, **Common**, **Pacific** and **Red-throated loons** may be seen, as well as **Horned**, **Western** and **Red-necked grebes** (very rarely **Eared Grebes**). **Soras**, **Virginia Rails**, **Pied-billed Grebes** and **Common Snipe** can at times be found in the marsh or ponds. **Great Blue Herons** are equally at home among the cattails, preening on a tall tree or fishing in the bay, but **Green Herons** are seen rarely. **Belted Kingfishers** regularly hunt along the ponds or from the wooden jetties of the Jericho Tennis Club and Royal Vancouver Yacht Club. **Sanderling** often scurry along the beach at the water's edge, sometimes joined by **Dunlin**. **Pelagic** and **Double-crested cormorants** may be seen on the bay. **Alcids** are not commonly found, though **Marbled Murrelets** do occur sporadically in winter.

In the less frequented upland area you may find **Red-tailed** and **Cooper's hawks**, and **Great Horned** and **Short-eared owls**. **Sharp-shinned Hawks** and **Merlins** also hunt here, and watch for **Bald Eagles** overhead or on snags. Now and then a **Northern Saw-whet** or **Barred owl** has made an appearance, but these are uncommon species for the park.

Varied Thrushes and **Northern Flickers** winter in the park, and the bramble thickets shelter **Song**, **White-crowned**, **Golden-crowned** and **Fox sparrows**, **House Finches** and other shrub-loving birds. Flocks of **Pine Siskins** and **American Goldfinches** feeding in the alder occasionally include a few **Common Redpolls** in the winter.

In summer (June and July) few songbirds remain other than **Red-winged Blackbirds**, **sparrows** and **finches**. Five species of **swallows** (**Barn**, **Cliff**, **Tree**, **Violet-green** and **Northern Rough-winged**) frequent the ponds. Particularly on cool, cloudy days **Black** and **Vaux's swifts** may be seen. At low tide **Bald Eagles** stand with the gulls far out on the sandy flats.

Spring and fall bring many species through on migration. In spring, watch for mixed feeding flocks of small passerines moving through the woodlots on the eastern side of the park near the ponds, among the trees bordering 4th Avenue and along the Pipeline Trail (which runs along the south side of the west marsh). These flocks may include **Wilson's**, **Yellow-rumped**, **Orange-crowned**, **Yellow** and occasionally **Black-throated Gray** and **Townsend's warblers**, **Warbling Vireos**, **Ruby-crowned** and **Golden-crowned kinglets** and **Black-capped Chickadees**. **Rufous Hummingbirds** visit the early salmonberry flowers. **Pacific-slope**, **Hammond's** and **Willow** are the most likely **flycatcher species** to be seen. **Cinnamon** and **Blue-winged teal** touch down on the ponds for a few days in spring.

Small numbers of shorebirds visit the ponds, especially in return migration (July onwards), when the water levels fall and the mud is exposed. These may include **Long-billed Dowitchers**, **Pectoral Sandpipers** and **Greater** and **Lesser yellowlegs**. **Band-tailed Pigeons** and **Lincoln's** and **Savannah sparrows** pass through the park. The long-grass meadow south of the concrete wharf may be visited briefly by small numbers of **Western Meadowlarks**, **Horned Larks**, **Snow Buntings** and **Lapland Longspurs** in fall migration, while **American Pipits** prefer the short-grass area north of the ponds. **Gulls** to be found around the pond or on the bay include **Glaucous-winged**, **Mew**, **Ring-billed**, **California**, **Thayer's** and **Bonaparte's**. In late September and early October a few **Franklin's Gulls** are usually seen off the crab pier west of the sailing centre, as are **Common Terns**.

About 20 species breed in the park, including *Willow Flycatchers*, *Cedar Waxwings*, *Bushtits*, *Song* and *White-crowned sparrows*, *Spotted Towhees*, *American Robins*, *Common Yellowthroats*, *Mallards*, *American Coots*, *Pied-billed Grebes* and *Barn* and *Violet-green swallows*. In total, some 180 species or more are found regularly in the park, and over the years more than 30 accidental species have been recorded.

Written and revised by Daphne Solecki

4. Queen Elizabeth Park

Queen Elizabeth Park is located near the centre of the City of Vancouver on Little Mountain, one of the highest hills in the city. Atop the hill is the Bloedel Floral Conservatory, a popular Vancouver tourist attraction, which features a dome that houses a wide variety of tropical and desert flora and a selection of tropical birds. The area was a rock quarry in the early part of the century. When the quarry ceased production it was turned into these magnificent gardens, and the park was named after Queen Elizabeth, the Queen Mother.

From the perimeter of the conservatory you have a panoramic view of the area. To the north are the mountains with the Cypress, Grouse and Seymour ski areas; downtown; the harbour and Stanley Park. To the west are the University of British Columbia, Pacific Spirit Regional Park and the Gulf Islands. Looking south, you see the lowlands of the Fraser delta, and to the east are Burnaby Mountain and Central Park.

Native trees in the park include Douglas-fir, western redcedar, western hemlock and vine maple. There is a large array of introduced trees and shrubs as well as several grassy areas and the quarry gardens—a magnificent display of flowering plants that provides a popular backdrop for wedding photos.

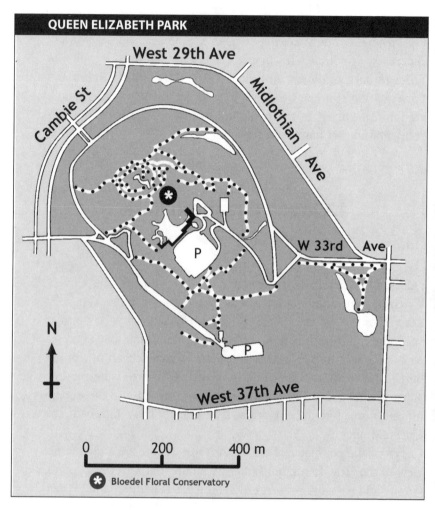

QUEEN ELIZABETH PARK

West 29th Ave

Cambie St

Midlothian Ave

W 33rd Ave

P

N

P

West 37th Ave

0   200   400 m

* Bloedel Floral Conservatory

Directions

To reach the park from downtown Vancouver, drive south on Cambie Street to 33rd Avenue, turn left, proceed for about 160 m (25 ft) and turn left again into the parking lot. There is also a ring road that circles around the north side of the park and goes up to another parking lot that sits atop a major water storage reservoir. These are both pay parking lots, but free parking is also available along roads. Check the regulations carefully before leaving your car.

Queen Elizabeth Park is also easily reached by the #15 Cambie bus from downtown Vancouver.

Bird Species

Time of day, season and weather play a major part in birding in Queen Elizabeth Park. On a pleasant sunny afternoon the park can be virtually devoid of birds. The best time of the year is mid-April through late May. The best time of day is usually early morning, although late afternoons can sometimes be productive. The best weather is bad weather—overcast skies, preferably following a storm, can provide an abundance of passerines all around the park.

This park is one of the best spots in Vancouver for migrant passerines. *Hammond's*, *Willow* and *Pacific-slope flycatchers*, *Swainson's* and *Hermit thrushes*, *Cassin's* and *Warbling vireos*, *Yellow-rumped*, *Wilson's*, *Orange-crowned* and *Yellow warblers*, *Western Tanagers* and *Lincoln's Sparrows* are found regularly, as are *Townsend's* and *Black-throated Gray warblers*. Throughout the park watch the skies for *five species of swallows*, and on overcast days look for *Black* and *Vaux's swifts*. *Townsend's Solitaires* and *Nashville Warblers* are annual in the park in small numbers. *Red-naped Sapsuckers*, *Calliope Hummingbirds* and *Tennessee Warblers* are more rare, but worth looking for. These species are rarely seen elsewhere in the Vancouver area.

As you walk away from the lower parking lot, follow a pathway southeast along the base of the hillside. Look here for *Swainson's* and *Hermit thrushes* in the evergreens and *Golden-crowned* and *White-crowned sparrows* along the ground. A radio tower is located up the hillside where the pathway turns to the left. Continue around the south side of the Lawn Bowling Club. The shrubbery here can contain a variety of *warblers* (*Tennessee Warblers* have been observed here), *Black-headed Grosbeaks*, *thrushes* and *Townsend's Solitaires* in spring.

The deciduous trees to the east of the Lawn Bowling Club provide shelter for *Bushtits*, *Black-capped Chickadees*, *Ruby-crowned* and *Golden-crowned kinglets*, *Lincoln's Sparrows* and occasionally *Red Crossbills*.

Proceed northwards across the road to the area of the conservatory and restaurant. The deciduous trees below the restaurant can harbour *Yellow*, *Wilson's*, *Townsend's*, *Black-throated Gray* and *Orange-crowned warblers*. Watch the tops of the conifers for *Western Wood-Pewees*, *Olive-sided Flycatchers* and *Western Tanagers*.

Continue around northwest to the area of the quarry gardens. *Townsend's Solitaires* visit this part of the park every spring, and *Band-tailed Pigeons* can sometimes be seen in the treetops. Watch and listen for *Hammond's*, *Willow* and *Pacific-slope flycatchers* in spring migration.

Follow the pathway through the woods around the north and west sides of the gardens. This area can produce *Cassin's* and *Warbling vireos* as well as an array of *Yellow-rumped* and other *warblers* and *flycatchers*. Proceeding in a southeasterly direction will complete the circle, returning you to the parking lot.

Written and revised by Dale Jensen

5. Fraser River Park/Musqueam Marsh Nature Park/Blenheim Flats

In the southwest part of Vancouver, along the Fraser River from Granville Street to the Musqueam Indian Reserve, you will find the most rural area of the city. The diversity of habitats fosters an exceptional array of bird species.

There are two parks located here—Musqueam Marsh Nature Park to the west and Fraser River Park to the east. Between these two small parks are three golf courses and considerable private lands in the area known locally as Blenheim Flats, much of which contains small holdings accommodating stables, horse paddocks and garden centres. Up until the early 1980s most of the land south of SW Marine Drive was bush, complete with frog and salamander ponds and even snowshoe hares! Industrial, park and residential developments have since changed this area considerably.

The North Arm of the Fraser River is a major transportation corridor for log booms, barges and tugboats. As in most areas near rivers, dykes were built to channel the river and protect lowlands from flooding. The habitats include western redcedar and a red alder forest, thickets of mixed woods (including tall cottonwoods and Lombardy poplars) along the horse trail and dyke areas, and sloughs and horse pastures in the vicinity of Blenheim Flats and Musqueam Marsh Nature Park.

Fraser River Park is a relatively new park running west along 75th Avenue on a narrow strip of tidal river edge. It provides access to the Fraser River in a setting that attempts to recreate the original natural riparian habitats. A small marsh and tidal flats have been replanted with native vegetation. Thickets of blackberry, salmonberry, wild rose and snowberry provide food and shelter for **passerines**, and grasses and thistles have been planted to attract a variety of **finches** and **sparrows**. A boardwalk along the water's edge and a short pier make it easy to scan the river for **water birds**. Several clumps of tall cottonwoods tend to attract **warblers** in spring. Interpretive signs at intervals along the paths and an interpretive court at the east end of the park explain the history of the area and the many artifacts.

Depending on your pace and diversions, these areas can be birded in a couple of hours or you can take a full day. Fraser River Park and Heron Nature Trail in Musqueam Marsh Nature Park probably offer the best birding opportunities.

Directions

Car access to Fraser River Park is available via 75th Avenue west of Granville Street or at the foot of Angus Drive, turning south off SW Marine Drive. There are two small parking lots, washrooms and picnic tables here.

The #8 Granville bus from downtown takes you within easy walking distance of Fraser River Park. Get off at the 75th Avenue stop.

Blenheim Flats, a rural area of horse stables, paddocks and garden centres, is located near the foot of Blenheim Street, in the area known as Southlands. It is roughly bounded by SW Marine Drive, Blenheim Street, Macdonald Street and the North Arm of the Fraser River. There are golf courses to the east and west. Blenheim Flats is best birded on foot, walking along the relatively quiet residential streets and paying close attention to the pastures and shrubby areas.

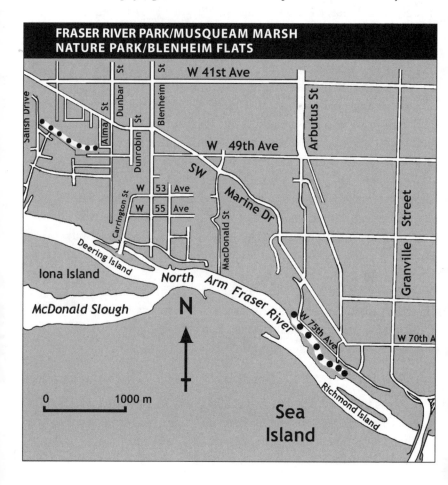

FRASER RIVER PARK/MUSQUEAM MARSH NATURE PARK/BLENHEIM FLATS

The 49th Avenue buses, mentioned below, come fairly close to this area. Consult a good map to study it in detail.

Heron Nature Trail in Musqueam Marsh Nature Park begins at the foot of Alma Street (one block west of Dunbar Street) and ends at Crown Street. There are no facilities here but there is limited street parking at the trailhead.

The 49th Avenue buses, #49 Dunbar Loop (westbound) or #49 Metrotown (eastbound), service this area. The eastbound bus stops at the corner of 49th Avenue and SW Marine Drive. Walk 1 block west to Alma Street, turn south (down a slight hill) and walk 2 blocks to the end of Alma to reach the east end of Heron Nature Trail (on your right).

Bird Species

Birding opportunities change with the season and habitat, but a good variety of species can always be found. The annual eulachon run (a small herring-like fish) occurs during April. The calls of **Bonaparte's Gulls** and occasionally **Common Terns** are a sure sign that eulachon are in the river. Other **gulls**, particularly **Glaucous-winged**, are attracted in numbers. Look for **Mew**, **Ring-billed**, **Herring**, **Thayer's** and other gull species among the loafing flocks settled on the log booms.

Double-crested Cormorants, **Common Loons**, **Western Grebes** and other fish-eating species including **Common** and **Red-breasted mergansers** are often seen on the river. Through the winter months smaller numbers of these species are represented.

Many of Vancouver's common waterfowl species will be found frequenting the sloughs and side channels. **Mallards**, **Green-winged Teal**, **Greater Scaup** and **Great Blue Herons** abound. Vegetated shoreline and drainage channels may shelter a **Green Heron**. **Killdeer** occur in the more open areas and **Spotted Sandpipers** frequent the river edge in summer.

Around the stables and in the horse paddocks, **Brewer's** and **Red-winged blackbirds** and **Brown-headed Cowbirds** are always present. Mixed flocks of these species gather, especially in winter. The horse paddocks occasionally sport a **Short-eared Owl** or two, and **Barn Owls** are reported to reside in some of the stables. **Ring-necked Pheasants** maintain a small population in this area. On the flats you may see raptors, including **Red-tailed Hawks**, **Bald Eagles** and **Cooper's** and **Sharp-shinned hawks**.

Musqueam Marsh Nature Park has long been known for its forest birds. **Black-capped** and **Chestnut-backed chickadees**, **Golden-crowned** and **Ruby-crowned kinglets**, **Red Crossbills**, **Hutton's Vireos**, **Hammond's Flycatchers** and **Western Wood-Pewees** are regulars in season. In the alder forest along the horse trail **Willow Flycatchers**, **Yellow** and other **warblers**, and **vireos** are summer residents. In winter, flocks of **Pine Siskins** (occasionally with **American Goldfinches** and **Common Redpolls** mixed in), **Fox** and **Song sparrows**, **Varied Thrushes**, **Dark-eyed Juncos** and **Spotted Towhees** frequent this habitat. **Evening Grosbeaks** are regular visitors to this area in spring and autumn. Looking for **Northern Saw-whet**, **Western Screech** and **Great Horned owls** in Musqueam Park can be particularly rewarding.

The horse trail, from near the west end of Heron Nature Trail towards the dyke, provides excellent birding during the spring migration period. The mixed forest/thicket habitats are excellent for **warblers**, **sparrows** and other small songbirds.

From June through July, **Black-headed Grosbeaks** and **Bullock's Orioles** are regular breeding species, but their numbers are very small. Tall birch thickets and Lombardy poplars, respectively, are the places to look for these species.

In past years this area of Vancouver has turned up some "firsts." A **Scrub Jay** appeared one fall and stayed for several weeks, and **Black-and-white Warblers** have occasionally been found here.

Written by Bill Merilees; revised by Catherine J. Aitchison

Crested Mynas in Vancouver

This bird, unique (in North America) to Vancouver, has maintained a small population in the city for over a century. Introduced in the 1890s, they flourished at first and flocks could be found in many parts of the city. In recent years, however, they have suffered a steady decline, possibly because of competition for nest sites from European Starlings. At the time of writing, the only reasonably reliable place to look for them is in central Vancouver, in the vicinity of Wylie Street between 1st and 2nd avenues (near the south end of the Cambie Street Bridge). This is an old industrial area of the city, with weathered brick buildings that have some holes and crevices in their outer walls.

In the spring breeding season, watch the west face of the building at 1921 Wylie (corner of 1st and Wylie), which bears the large sign "Best Janitors and Building Maintenance." In recent years, the birds have nested in a cavity in the brick wall. To the left of the double doors on the third floor and below the "t" in "Janitors," there is a short pipe protruding from the wall. The mynas go in and out through the pipe. They also perch on the black bracket between the double doors and the window to the left.

Outside of the breeding season, mynas could be anywhere in the area, possibly roaming as far as four or five blocks away. Check the numerous overhead wires and the roof edges of nearby buildings, as well as the public works yard on the north side of 1st Avenue. The best tactic is to walk or drive around the immediate area, paying particular attention to the west wall of 1921 Wylie. Listen for the mynas' loud, raucous vocalization. Early morning or near sunset are probably the best times of day to see them.

Mynas have also been reported recently from the area around 70th Avenue and Hudson Street, but this is now a far less reliable area than Wylie Street. A stroll down back alleys behind the shops will provide the best opportunities. The rooftops and boulevards in the vicinity of 73rd Avenue and Hudson are worth checking, and, in the recent past, the birds have nested in a hollow pipe in the sign on the Arthur Laing Bridge.

Written by Jo Ann MacKenzie and Catherine J. Aitchison

Vancouver Natural History Society
P.O. Box 3021, Vancouver, B.C. V6B 3X5
Events and Information, and **Bird Alert**
Tel: (604) 737-3074, 24 hours a day

North and West Vancouver

6. Maplewood Conservation Area

The Maplewood Conservation Area in North Vancouver is the last undeveloped waterfront wetland on the north shore of Burrard Inlet. For over 20 years, public interest groups lobbied to preserve this prime site as a wildlife sanctuary. In 1992 the owners of the majority of the area (the federal government's Vancouver Port Authority, or VPA) reached an agreement to lease the VPA area for 49 years to Environment Canada to permit the area to be managed as a wildlife conservation area. In the late 1980s, the District of North Vancouver (DNV), which owns important fresh and saltwater marshlands adjoining the VPA lands, designated the DNV and VPA lands as the Maplewood Conservation Area in a motion by council.

The VPA, the DNV and Environment Canada chose WBT Wild Bird Trust of B.C. as the operators of the Conservation Area. WBT, a membership-based provincial organization, was founded by Dr. Richard C. Beard and Patricia Banning-Lover in 1993. Dedicated to the protection of birds and their habitats on the principle that all wildlife must benefit, the WBT met the challenge of turning a former industrial site into a haven for wildlife. The organization regards the conservation area at Maplewood Flats as its flagship sanctuary—thousands of volunteer hours have been spent on restoration, and the dream of evolving a "living classroom" for all to enjoy is finally coming true. Landscape architect Patrick Mooney designed all the major enhancement projects at Maplewood, including the freshwater marsh. Over 3 km (1.9 mi) of wheelchair-accessible trails, with occasional resting benches, have been constructed in the area to permit the public to observe the abundant wildlife. Future plans include a Nature House and self-guided trail brochure.

From August through October, black bears arrive in the area to eat mountain ash berries and blackberries. Keep to the trails and make noise (rattle keys, talk, etc.); the bears normally remove themselves into the bushes (see page 63). Other species that may be seen are coast mule deer, coyotes, harbour seals, river otters, mink, weasels, skunks, raccoons, squirrels and, very occasionally, a bobcat or a cougar. *Do not feed these mammals*—leave them to get on with their lives.

Directions

The Maplewood Conservation Area is east of the north end of the Ironworkers Memorial (Second Narrows) Bridge on the south side of the Dollarton Highway. From downtown Vancouver, drive east via Hastings or McGill streets to the bridge, which crosses Burrard Inlet to North Vancouver. Take the Dollarton Highway (Deep Cove) exit #23B and proceed for approximately 3 km (1.9 mi) to 2645 Dollarton Highway (on the right). This is the entrance to both the Maplewood Conservation Area and Environment Canada's Pacific Environmental Science Centre. This is the only entrance to the area, and visitor parking is provided here at the following times: Monday through Friday 7 A.M. to 6 P.M.; Saturday and Sunday 9:30 A.M. to 4 P.M. *Note: The Environment Canada gate closes automatically at closing time.* Visitors should plan their parking accordingly, especially on weekends, when staff members are not always available to unlock the gate for latecomers returning to the parking lot. Alternative parking is available on the north side of the highway between the Canadian International College and the Crab Shop.

The Maplewood Conservation Area can be reached by public transit from downtown Vancouver via the #210 Upper Lynn Valley bus going east on Pender Street. Proceed to Phibbs Exchange and transfer to either a #211 or #212 going east on Dollarton Highway. Alternatively, take the SeaBus to Lonsdale Quay and transfer to the

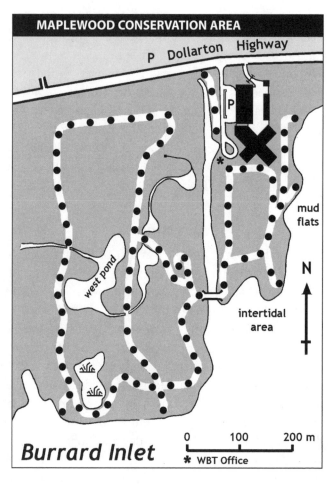

#239 Capilano College bus to Phibbs Exchange. Then transfer to a #211 or #212 bus and ask to be let off on Dollarton Highway, in the area of the Canadian International College and the Crab Shop.

Bird Species

The mix of six habitat types at the Maplewood Conservation Area has attracted over 220 species of birds in the past 25 years. Thus, the species to be expected are grouped by habitat.

INTERTIDAL FLATS AND SALT MARSH

Flats to the south, west and east are most extensive on the eastern side, with shingle, gravel and mud bars to the south and a smaller area of mud, gravel and cobble flats to the west. The flats have 37 groupings of old poles (called dolphins), which were used for log boom storage. The tidal flats are fully exposed only at low tide; at high tide, the salt marsh fringe is also flooded. In winter this zone is a major feeding ground for flocks of **American Wigeon** (often with a **Eurasian Wigeon**), **Green-winged Teal**, **Dunlin** and **Mew Gulls** with smaller groups of **Gadwall**, **Northern Pintails**, **Hooded** and **Common mergansers**, **Greater Yellowlegs**, **Long-billed Dowitchers** and **Black Turnstones**. The high-tide line attracts flocks of up to 20 **Red Crossbills**, which eat salt and other trace minerals. March through May brings **Cinnamon** and **Blue-winged teal** and various **plovers**, **sandpipers** and **gulls**. Starting in July, these species begin their fall migration. **Black-bellied Plovers**, **Least**, **Western**, **Baird's**, **Pectoral**, **Stilt** and **Semipalmated sandpipers**, **Red-necked** and **Wilson's phalaropes**, **dowitcher** and **yellowleg species**, **Whimbrels**, **Bonaparte's**, **Ring-billed** and **California gulls** and **Common Terns** might be seen at this time.

In summer, bachelor parties of **Harlequin Ducks** use the area, along with breeding **Ospreys**. A pair of Ospreys first nested at Maplewood in 1991, and up to four pairs now breed in Burrard Inlet. The Ospreys can be seen hunting over the shallows, sometimes in the company of **Caspian Terns**.

In 1992 a nest box project brought breeding **Purple Martins** back to the mainland of B.C. for the first time in 22 years. The nest boxes were attached to the dolphin post clusters, which stand in the mud flats and have saltwater around them much of the time. From a single nesting pair in 1994, the new colony grew to 22 pairs with eggs in their boxes by July 2000. There are over 80 nest boxes on the dolphins. Many of the adults have come from colonies on Vancouver Island and even Oregon. They arrive in early May and depart at the end of August, with a few remaining in the first week of September. You can most easily observe them in late July and

August in good weather, when they are hunting and in song flight over the conservation area, or with a scope when they're perched around their nest boxes. They are very defensive of their breeding sites and have been observed in aerial pursuit and attack on *Cooper's Hawks*, *Merlins*, *Glaucous-winged Gulls* and *Northwestern Crows*. The *Ospreys*, which use the tops of the dolphins for their nests, are generally not attacked by the *Purple Martins*.

DEEP SALTWATER BASIN

To the south of the rough meadow and freshwater marsh area is a deep saltwater basin that holds water at low tide and provides a deep-water feeding zone for hundreds of *Barrow's* and *Common goldeneyes*, *Surf Scoters* and *Greater Scaup*, with smaller numbers of *Horned Grebes*, *Pelagic Cormorants*, *Red-breasted Mergansers*, *Harlequin Ducks* and *Buffleheads* in winter. Unusual species in winter include *Red-throated Loons*, *Red-necked Grebes*, *Brandt's Cormorants*, *Long-tailed Ducks* and *Common Murres* in ones or twos. Late summer may provide sightings of *Common Terns* and *Parasitic Jaegers*.

FRESHWATER MARSH/PONDS SYSTEM

With funding secured by WBT from government, industry and the public, an extensive freshwater marsh and ponds system with interconnecting creeks was excavated in the 30-year-old filled area in the western part of the site. The system was dedicated in the spring of 1997 and is now a breeding habitat for *Marsh Wrens*, *Common Yellowthroats*, *Wood Ducks*, *American Coots*, *Blue-winged Teal*, *Red-winged Blackbirds*, *Pied-billed Grebes*, *Soras* and *Virginia Rails*. In spring, *Redheads*, *Canvasbacks*, *Lesser Scaup*, *Northern Shovelers*, *Yellow-headed Blackbirds* and *Cinnamon Teal* use the ponds. Fall brings many of these species back, with the additions of *Green Herons* and *Hooded Mergansers*. On summer evenings *Violet-green*, *Northern Rough-winged*, *Barn*, *Cliff* and *Tree swallows* feed over the pond where *Purple Martins* and *Vaux's* and

Black swifts join them when the weather is overcast. Directly to the west of the pond is a natural freshwater marsh/pond and salt marsh complex, which is a small example of the original shoreline habitat. It provides nesting sites for **Green Herons**, **Soras**, **Virginia Rails**, **Bewick's Wrens**, **Hutton's Vireos**, **Spotted Towhees** and **ducks**. From autumn through spring the marsh/pond complex is used by **ducks**, **Common Snipe**, **yellowlegs** and **dowitchers**, an occasional **American Bittern** and local **songbird species**.

OPEN ROUGH MEADOW

This area of 35-year-old filled-in mud flats is now breeding habitat for **American Goldfinches** and **Savannah** and **White-crowned sparrows**. During spring and fall migration, the meadows attract **American Kestrels**, **Western Meadowlarks**, **American Pipits**, **Western Bluebirds**, **Townsend's Solitaires** and **Eastern** and **Western kingbirds**. **Short-eared Owls**, **Northern Harriers** and **Rough-legged Hawks** also utilize the area in migration. In winter, **Northern Shrikes**, **Northern Pygmy-Owls** and **Merlins** hunt flocks of **finches**, **sparrows**, **robins** and **flickers** in the area. Unusual species to watch for at this season are **Snow Buntings**, **Lapland Longspurs** and **Common Snipe**.

BLACK COTTONWOOD—RED ALDER—SITKA SPRUCE FORESTS

The northwest and northeast portions of the site have remnant deciduous (on the west) and mixed coniferous-deciduous (on the east) riparian forests. In spring and autumn these trees are feeding habitat for migrating **warblers**, **vireos**, **flycatchers**, **tanagers** and **thrushes**. In summer, look for breeding **Black-headed Grosbeaks**, **Western Tanagers**, **Swainson's Thrushes** and **Warbling**, **Cassin's** and **Red-eyed vireos**. In winter, **Red-breasted Sapsuckers**, **Hairy Woodpeckers**, **Hutton's Vireos** and **Hermit Thrushes** may be seen with the flocks of **Golden-crowned** and **Ruby-crowned kinglets**, **Black-capped Chickadees** and **Brown Creepers**. Groups of **Varied Thrushes** and **Spotted Towhees** forage in the leaf litter. In the western coniferous (Sitka spruce, western redcedar, Douglas-fir and western hemlock) and deciduous forest, *Chestnut-backed Chickadees*, *Red-breasted Nuthatches*, *Red Crossbills*, *Pileated Woodpeckers* and *Steller's Jays* can be added to the winter mix of species.

BRAMBLE—RED ALDER—MOUNTAIN ASH— PACIFIC CRABAPPLE SHRUB ZONE

Much of the eastern zone and scattered areas throughout the site are covered by a mixed-species shrub and small-tree habitat. This provides breeding sites for *Cedar Waxwings*, *Western Wood-Pewees*, *Bushtits*, *Spotted Towhees*, *Rufous Hummingbirds*, *Purple Finches* and *Yellow* and *MacGillivray's warblers*. In winter, flocks of *Pine Siskins* (watch for a possible *Common Redpoll*), *Evening Grosbeaks* (common in some winters), *Purple* and *House finches* and *Varied Thrushes* feed on the bramble, alder and other seeds and berries. *Bewick's Wrens*, *Hutton's Vireos*, *Fox Sparrows*, *Downy Woodpeckers* and *Ruby-crowned Kinglets* also use these thickets. *Band-tailed Pigeons* feed here from March through October.

Sharp-shinned, *Cooper's* and *Red-tailed hawks*, *Bald Eagles*, *Peregrine Falcons*, *Merlins*, *Barred Owls* and *Great Horned Owls* use the whole area. *Great Blue Herons*, *Belted Kingfishers*, *Common Loons*, *Glaucous-winged Gulls* and *Killdeer* are year-round residents. *Turkey Vultures* hunt over the area in summer.

Written by Kevin Bell; revised by Kevin Bell and Patricia M. Banning-Lover

7. Lighthouse Park and Vicinity

Lighthouse Park is located in West Vancouver, a short drive from downtown Vancouver. Point Atkinson, the rocky headland on which it is situated, was named after Thomas Atkinson, a Royal Navy captain, by Captain George Vancouver while he was engaged in survey work on the southern British Columbia coast in 1792.

In 1873–74 the first lighthouse was built to protect ships sailing to logging camps and sawmills on the shores of Burrard Inlet. The stone base of this old wooden tower is still visible to the west of the present lighthouse. In 1881 the 75 ha (185 a) of crown land to the north of the lighthouse was granted to the Dominion government for a lighthouse reserve. In 1910 the reserve was leased to North Vancouver and then leased to West Vancouver upon its incorporation in 1912.

Today's Lighthouse Park has remained relatively undisturbed. It contains a remarkable range of natural conditions and varied environments. Approximately two-thirds of the park's perimeter is shoreline consisting of coves, rocky headlands, high granite cliffs and a group of small rocky islands to the northwest of the park. Trees and shrubs, such as arbutus, shore pine and salal, thrive here.

The interior of the park is punctuated by high, rounded granite outcrops, up to almost 120 m (394 ft) above sea level. Between them are valleys and narrow draws where deeper soil supports a magnificent coniferous forest. The largest trees are Douglas-fir, some over 400 years old, 60 m (197 ft) high and 2 m (6 ft) in diameter. Other tree species include western hemlock and western redcedar, with lesser numbers of bigleaf maple and red alder. The shaded forest floor is covered with red huckleberry, sword fern, western hemlock seedlings and thickets of salmonberry as well as colonies of Oregon grape, deer fern and various mosses.

A ubiquitous resident in Lighthouse Park is the Douglas squirrel, a tiny, golden-brown creature often mistaken by visitors for a chipmunk. Douglas squirrels are the only west coast native species.

The best location to view **shorebirds** in this area is actually outside Lighthouse Park, in another small park just to the west. This is Klootchman Park (described below), which consists mainly of a trail with a steep set of staircases leading down through the forest from the top of the cliff to Indian Bluff, a rocky lookout facing the Grebe Islets (about 15 minutes' walk). Try to visit on a low tide, which exposes feeding sites on the islets, and use a scope to obtain the best views. If you don't want to tackle stairs carrying your scope, you can still obtain a view of the Grebe Islets from Pitcairn Place (described below), a cul-de-sac from which it is possible to use a scope. *Stay on the roadway here and do not trespass.*

Directions

To reach Lighthouse Park from Vancouver, drive north over the Lions Gate Bridge and take the exit to West Vancouver (at this point you will be driving west on Marine Drive). The first traffic light is at the intersection of Marine Drive and Taylor Way. Go straight through this intersection and follow Marine Drive west for 10.3 km (6.4 mi) to Beacon Lane (watch carefully for the small Lighthouse Park sign on your left). Turn left on Beacon Lane and follow it for .3 km (.2 mi) to the park gate and parking area. Alternatively, you can take the Ironworkers Memorial (Second Narrows) Bridge north from East Vancouver or Burnaby to North Vancouver. Continue west on the Upper Levels Highway (Highway 1 West) to the Taylor Way exit (#13), then turn left on Taylor Way, drive south to the intersection with Marine Drive, turn right and proceed as above.

Lighthouse Park is easy to reach by bus from downtown Vancouver. From Georgia Street, take the westbound #250 Horseshoe Bay bus and ask the driver to let you off at the stop closest to the park entrance. *Do not* take the #257 Horseshoe Bay Express, which does not stop there.

Bird Species

Over 150 bird species have been recorded in the park. There is a good variety of opportunities for viewing both sea and land birds, but because of the rugged terrain visitors must be prepared and alert. Sturdy footwear will allow you to explore the many steep, rocky trails, while common sense will keep you a safe distance from steep cliffs.

Lush ground cover in the interior of the park is a favourite haunt of *Song Sparrows*, *Spotted Towhees*, *Dark-eyed Juncos* and *Winter Wrens*. As you walk the trails listen for *Red-breasted Nuthatches*, *Bushtits*, *Varied Thrushes* and *Hutton's Vireos* (most vocal from February to April). The three large open areas (the parking lot, the area near the outdoor theatre and along the service road) are good locations from which to search the forest canopy for *Band-tailed Pigeons*, *Purple Finches*, *Evening Grosbeaks*, *Pine Siskins* and *Red Crossbills*. Early spring arrivals include *Violet-green Swallows* (February) and *Rufous Hummingbirds*

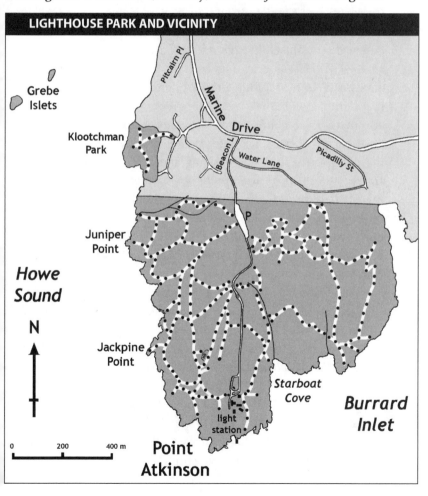

LIGHTHOUSE PARK AND VICINITY

Grebe Islets

Klootchman Park

Pitcairn Pl

Marine Drive

Beacon L

Water Lane

Picadilly St

P

Juniper Point

Howe Sound

N

Jackpine Point

Starboat Cove

Burrard Inlet

light station

0   200   400 m

Point Atkinson

(March), while species such as **Western Tanagers** and **Swainson's Thrushes** arrive later in May. Four species of *flycatchers* summer in the park. **Hammond's** and **Pacific-slope flycatchers** prefer the deep forest, **Western Wood-Pewees** prefer slightly more open areas, and **Olive-sided Flycatchers** will often be found high on a conifer snag. **Common Ravens**, **Northwestern Crows** and **Steller's Jays** are the resident corvid species. **Brown Creepers**, **Chestnut-backed Chickadees** and **Golden-crowned Kinglets** are park residents and, in winter, form mixed flocks along with the occasional wintering **Ruby-crowned Kinglet**. Breeding **warblers** include **Townsend's** and **Black-throated Grays** high in the trees, while **Wilson's**, **Orange-crowned** and **MacGillivray's** are found in the understory. **Yellow-rumped Warblers** occur only as transients. In early spring one is almost sure to hear a **Blue Grouse** booming. Since these birds tend to call from high in the trees where they are difficult to see, it can be advantageous to climb a granite outcrop (carefully!) near a calling bird to gain a better view into the tree canopy. Check the snags in the park, as they provide foraging and breeding sites for **Downy**, **Hairy** and **Pileated woodpeckers**, **Northern Flickers** and **Red-breasted Sapsuckers**. The park offers the opportunity to view a few birds of prey, such as **Bald Eagles**, *accipiters* and **Northern Pygmy-Owls**, which often call during the daylight hours. On a nocturnal visit you might observe **Great Horned**, **Barred**, **Western Screech** or **Northern Saw-whet owls**.

The cliffs and rock bluffs of the park provide many excellent sites to scan for birds on the water. **Common Loons** are abundant in winter, while **Red-throated** and **Pacific loons** also winter here but occur in lesser numbers. Careful searching of the **loons** might produce a **Yellow-billed Loon**, which is a rare winter visitor to Vancouver waters. Of the **gulls** that can be seen in the park, **Glaucous-winged Gulls** are year-round residents. There are **Mew** (some summering birds), **Thayer's** and a few **Herring gulls** present in the winter. Look for **Bonaparte's Gulls** from April to November and **Common Terns** during the spring and fall migrations. **Alcids** can also be found in the offshore waters. **Pigeon Guillemots** and

Marbled Murrelets are park residents, although the Marbled Murrelets' numbers are declining. *Common Murres* are rare in the winter, and *Rhinoceros Auklets* (summer) and *Ancient Murrelets* (winter) are both scarce, but are occasionally observed.

Klootchman Park and Pitcairn Place
Directions

To reach these two areas from Lighthouse Park, return to Marine Drive and turn left. The first left turn is Howe Sound Lane, leading to Klootchman Park. The trail to Klootchman Park begins just past The Byway on your right. (Look very carefully for the sign—it may be overgrown by foliage in the summer.) Parking is extremely limited here—make sure you don't park in a driveway or private parking space. The second left turn west of Lighthouse Park is Pitcairn Place.

Bird Species

Black Oystercatchers are residents of the Grebe Islets and are joined during the winter by large numbers of *Surfbirds*, *Black Turnstones* and a few *Rock Sandpipers*. From Indian Bluff, look for rafts of *Western Grebes* as well as *Red-necked* and *Horned grebes*, which congregate near the islets during the winter. *Double-crested* and *Pelagic cormorants* are residents, while *Brandt's Cormorants* occur only in small numbers during the winter. *Harlequin Ducks* and *Surf Scoters* can usually be seen all year round (smaller numbers during the summer) and are joined by *Greater Scaup*, *Buffleheads*, *Barrow's* and *Common goldeneyes*, *White-winged* and *Black scoters* and *Red-breasted Mergansers* during the winter months. *Wandering Tattlers* are uncommon, but try looking for them during migration in the late summer or early fall. If you observe the Grebe Islets from Pitcairn Place, check the residential plantings for *Anna's Hummingbirds* (resident) and *Townsend's Solitaires* (spring migrants).

Written and revised by Danny Tyson

8. Ambleside Park

Ambleside Park is a small, urban waterfront park in West Vancouver, across the Lions Gate Bridge from downtown Vancouver. It faces Stanley Park across the waters of the First Narrows of Burrard Inlet. With the right weather conditions, Ambleside Park can be an excellent place to see migrant birds. The park contains many different habitats, which include a pond and golf course surrounded by ornamental plantings, a rocky foreshore, a tidal river mouth and mixed second-growth woodland. These varied habitats have been host to many vagrant species in the Vancouver area. The park is used heavily by the public and is quite often overrun by dog walkers. To avoid dogs, an early-morning start is essential.

Directions

To reach Ambleside Park from Vancouver, drive north over the Lions Gate Bridge and take the exit to West Vancouver. This exit will lead you to a traffic light at Marine Drive and Taylor Way. Alternatively, you can take the Ironworkers Memorial (Second Narrows) Bridge north from East Vancouver or Burnaby to North Vancouver. Continue west on the Upper Levels Highway (Highway 1 West) to exit #13, Taylor Way, then turn left on Taylor Way and proceed south to Marine Drive. From the light at Taylor Way and Marine Drive, follow Marine Drive west past the Park Royal Shopping Centre to 13th Street. Turn left (south), cross the railway tracks and turn left (east) again into Ambleside Park. Park in the farthest east parking lot. Directly opposite the parking lot is the Ambleside pond.

It takes less than 15 minutes to reach Ambleside Park by bus from downtown Vancouver. Take the #250 Horseshoe Bay bus (*not* the #257 Horseshoe Bay Express) westbound on Georgia Street to 13th Street in West Vancouver and walk across the railway tracks towards the water, into the park.

Bird Species

The Ambleside pond should be checked from September to May for **Ring-necked Ducks** among the numerous **Greater** and **Lesser scaup**. Other waterfowl usually present include **Mallards**, **Canvasbacks**, **Common Goldeneyes**, **Buffleheads** and the occasional **Hooded Merganser** or **Pied-billed Grebe**. **American Wigeon** frequent the grass playing fields near the pond and are often accompanied by one or two **Eurasian Wigeon**. The rare **Tufted Duck** has been seen several times in the pond in winter.

Songbirds are attracted to the ornamental plantings surrounding the pond and rough areas to the east. These sites can sometimes be alive with migrant passerines, although they are normally quiet. Common residents include **Bushtits**, **Northwestern Crows**, **House Finches**, **Red-winged Blackbirds**, **Winter Wrens**, **Black-capped Chickadees** and **White-crowned** and **Song sparrows**. You may also encounter **Red Crossbills** in winter, but sightings are sporadic.

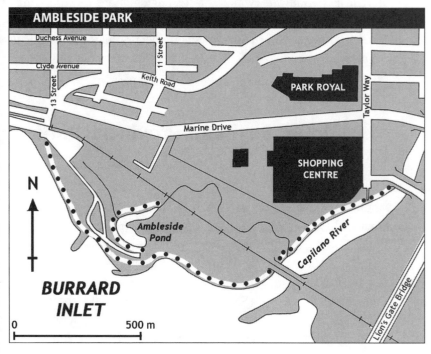

After checking the pond, walk south to a small rocky spit that juts out into Burrard Inlet. From fall through spring (October to March) large numbers of **Surf Scoters** and **Barrow's Goldeneyes** congregate, with lesser numbers of **Long-tailed Ducks** and **White-winged** and **Black scoters** mixed in. Other birds present on the water include **Common** and **Red-throated loons**, **Red-necked**, **Horned** and **Western grebes**, **Double-crested** and **Pelagic cormorants**, and occasional **Brandt's Cormorants**, **Harlequin Ducks**, **Red-breasted Mergansers** and **Pigeon Guillemots**. **Marbled Murrelets** are sometimes seen, but are rare.

During low tides, gravel bars are exposed and can be viewed from the spit. Check the flocks of **Glaucous-winged** and **Mew gulls** for **Thayer's**, **Herring**, **Western** (rare) and **Glaucous gulls** (rare) in the winter, and **California Gulls** in the spring and fall.

Follow the shoreline east from here to reach the Capilano River. This can be a good spot to see **Great Blue Herons**, **Common Mergansers**, **Gadwall** (winter), **Bald Eagles**, more roosting **gulls**, **Belted Kingfishers** (usually around the railway bridge) and **Northern Rough-winged Swallows** (summer). Sometimes **American Dippers** can also be found wintering in the lower stretch of the river.

Written and revised by Danny Tyson

9. Mount Seymour Provincial Park

Mount Seymour Provincial Park in North Vancouver and Cypress Provincial Park in West Vancouver provide the most accessible sub-alpine birding in the Vancouver area. Mount Seymour Provincial Park is a 3,508-ha (8,668-a) mountain wilderness bounded on the east by Indian Arm, on the south by the municipality of North Vancouver, on the west by the Seymour River and the Greater Vancouver Water District watershed and on the north by the Coast Mountains. The park includes most of Mount Seymour and nearby

Mount Elsay and Mount Bishop, all of which are over 1,400 m (4,593 ft) high.

Much of the original coastal hemlock forest, which is found at elevations below 1,000 m (3,300 ft), was logged in the 1920s. The resultant second-growth forest is a mixture of deciduous (mostly red alder) and coniferous (mostly western hemlock) trees. At elevations above 1,000 m, characteristic plants of the coastal subalpine forest predominate. No logging took place in this higher area, so there are significant areas of old-growth mountain hemlock and yellow-cedar. The trees and associated shrubs—copperbush and white rhododendron—tend to grow in "islands" separated by shrubs such as red heather and blueberry.

Sitka mountain-ash berries are an important food for birds in the subalpine zone. This area contains a number of water-related habitats, including bog vegetation fringing Goldie and Flower lakes. Open water is limited mainly to the larger lakes such as Goldie Lake and, in the backcountry, Elsay Lake, which has been stocked with trout.

Ski runs in the park are covered with sparse pioneer vegetation, such as saxifrage and partridgefoot. This habitat is a factor of some importance to bird species such as **Blue Grouse**, which roost in nearby trees but feed along the forest edges and ski slopes in summer and fall.

Directions

To reach Mount Seymour from downtown Vancouver, drive east via Hastings or McGill streets to the Ironworkers Memorial (Second Narrows) Bridge, which crosses Burrard Inlet to North Vancouver. Take the Mount Seymour exit, which leads you to the right and onto Mount Seymour Parkway. Continue for about 7 km (4 mi) to Mount Seymour Road. Turn left here and continue ahead. A sign directs you to the park office near the entrance, where bird checklists, maps and other information are available Monday to Friday during normal business hours.

It is 10 km (6.2 mi), via a paved highway, from the park entrance at 100 m (330 ft) elevation to the topmost parking area at 1,000 m (3,300 ft). At 850 m (2,800 ft) elevation, Deep Cove Lookout provides a scenic viewpoint. A network of hiking trails begins at the upper parking lots. Two suggested routes for birders are Goldie Lake with associated ponds and bog vegetation (1 to 1 1/2 hours return) and Mystery Peak, including Mystery Lake (about 2 hours return, and an elevation change of 450 m/1,485 ft).

The weather can change very rapidly on a mountaintop. Be prepared by taking warm clothing and/or raingear with you. Wear good hiking boots and stay on the trails.

Bird Species

About 126 species, of which 14 are accidentals, have been recorded in Mount Seymour Provincial Park. The park checklist indicates that occurrences of particular species are markedly seasonal and keyed to altitude.

Most of the park's specialty birds are subalpine species. **Blue Grouse** are seen at all elevations, commonly along the roadsides. A good time to see them is spring (May and June), when they are hooting. Hens with broods are often seen in the summer. Blue Grouse, which live high up in trees, migrate to higher altitudes in winter. Tracks in the snow are a good clue to their presence. **Rock** and **White-tailed ptarmigan** are recent regular additions to the park species list. Mount Seymour is now "the" place to find these birds in winter, especially in the valleys between Mystery Peak and Second Pump Peak. Look for **Gray-crowned Rosy-Finches** in winter (November to March) in the subalpine regions. Flocks can be seen along roadsides feeding on seeds.

Species typical of the lower coastal hemlock forest in summer are **Swainson's Thrushes**, **Black-headed Grosbeaks**, **Warbling Vireos** and **Western Tanagers**. The common resident birds include **Winter Wrens**, **Varied Thrushes** and **Chestnut-backed Chickadees**. In the mountain hemlock regions, common summer residents

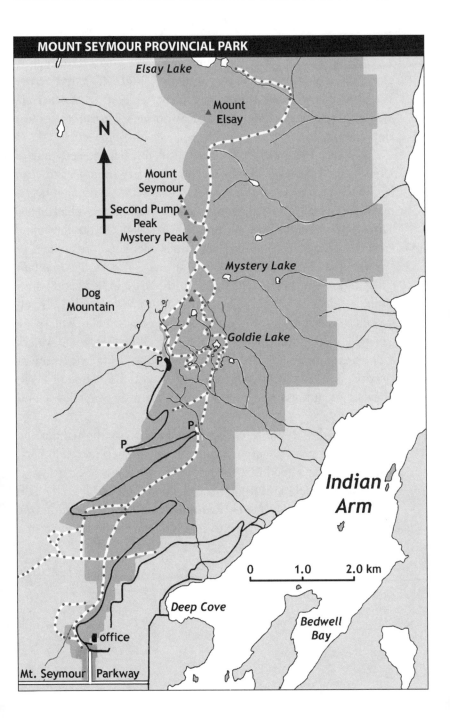

include **Hermit Thrushes** and **Vaux's Swifts**.

Bird species of lower elevations may be seen to have higher-elevation counterparts. For example, **Black-throated Gray Warblers** of the lower slopes tend to be replaced by **Townsend's Warblers** at higher elevations. The **Swainson's Thrushes** of lower slopes are replaced by **Hermit Thrushes** in subalpine areas.

Northern Pygmy-Owls are park residents, but the best time to look for this species is in winter. Numbers vary from year to year. Look along roadsides and trailsides, where they often perch in the open. They feed on small birds such as **kinglets** and **chickadees**. **Three-toed Woodpeckers** are probably residents in the subalpine area. Goldie Lake and Mystery Lake trails offer good possibilities to see them and, along the way, you may also find **Mountain Chickadees**. You might find **Pine Grosbeaks**, another winter sub-alpine resident, at Mystery Peak. **Gray Jays** will probably find you if you eat your lunch in the park! **Chestnut-backed Chickadees** are generally distributed throughout the park. Both **Black** and **Vaux's swifts** are summer residents here. Good places to see swifts are at Deep Cove Lookout on the main highway and at Mystery Peak. They are often present in good numbers when there is a low cloud ceiling.

Both **Red** and **White-winged crossbills** occur throughout the park; the former are more regular in occurrence and numbers. Mystery Peak is a good place to find both species.

Be on the lookout during migration times, especially in the fall, for raptors such as **accipiters**, **Red-tailed** and **Rough-legged hawks** and **falcons**. A fairly easy hike to Dog Mountain will bring you to a good, open lookout for a hawk watch.

Written and revised by Al Grass

10. Cypress Provincial Park

Cypress Provincial Park in West Vancouver and Mount Seymour Provincial Park in North Vancouver provide the most accessible subalpine birding in the Vancouver area. Cypress Provincial Park, established in 1975 and now almost 3,000 ha (7,410 a) in size, forms part of the North Shore mountains, the scenic backdrop to Vancouver. An excellent paved road climbs through western hemlock and Douglas-fir forests, eventually reaching more level terrain near the headwaters of Cypress Creek at an elevation of 1,000 m (3,300 ft). At this point you are in the lower reaches of the coastal subalpine forest, known to biologists as the Mountain Hemlock Zone. This zone is famous for its huge accumulations of snow in winter and subsequent late snowmelt in spring—and often early summer! Characteristic trees are mountain hemlock, yellow-cedar, amabilis fir and western white pine. Plants such as red heather, blueberry, huckleberry, false azalea, white rhododendron and copperbush dominate the understory. A number of small lakes and fens add to the natural diversity, and much of the remaining forest is beautiful old growth, with many large trees and snags.

Views are excellent from several places in the park, especially for the more adventurous birders who climb one of the three peaks. Large clear-cut areas detract greatly from the scenic beauty, but provide summer habitat for ***Blue Grouse***.

Directions

From downtown Vancouver, drive west on Georgia Street and cross the Lions Gate Bridge, following signs to West Vancouver. At the first traffic light, bear right onto Taylor Way. Follow this street up the hill and watch for signs indicating the Upper Levels Highway (Highway 1). Turn left (west) onto the Upper Levels and continue to the Cypress Provincial Park exit. The road starts at 300 m (984 ft) elevation, climbs gently at first to a tight corner, then more steeply to a second switchback at Hi-View Lookout. This is about 5.3 km (3.3 mi) from the highway at an elevation of 525 m (1,723 ft). After a stop here, continue up the hill around two more switchback corners, past the cross-country ski area, until you reach the end of the road at the Cypress Bowl downhill ski area. The ski operations are owned and operated by Cypress Bowl Recreations, Ltd., who also provide cafeteria service most of the year. Washrooms are located in the cafeteria building at the main parking lot. You have several options once you reach the parking area; indeed, there is a myriad of trails in this park.

The Yew Lake Trail, an easy 1.5-km (.9-mi) loop, makes a good starting point. Starting at the bases of both chairlifts, this trail follows Cypress Creek through open forest to Yew Lake. At a small fen system near the lake, a boardwalk trail leads north into a patch of forest and then out onto a logging road in a burn area. A short walk to the northwest here provides a good view of Howe Sound and excellent birding, especially during fall migration.

The Howe Sound Crest Trail starts at the same point as the Yew Lake Trail, but branches off to the right (north) just past the Mount Strachan chairlift, climbing the ridge quickly and eventually leading (after a long and strenuous hike) to the Lions, perhaps Vancouver's most scenic mountains. Only experienced hikers with a good map should attempt the hike to the Lions; the trail is not maintained for the length of the ridge.

A section of the Baden-Powell Trail leads from the parking lot up the slopes of Black Mountain (1,217 m/3,992 ft), where another loop trail winds around some small subalpine lakes. Another popular hike is up Hollyburn Mountain (1,325 m/4,347 ft), which can be reached from the cross-country ski area.

Bird Species

Cypress is best visited from May through October. Make the Hi-View Lookout your first stop. It not only offers a magnificent vista

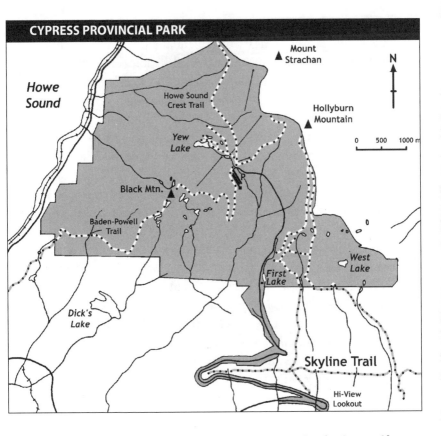

CYPRESS PROVINCIAL PARK

of Vancouver (and, on a clear day, Vancouver Island, the Gulf Islands and the North Cascade Mountains), but is also a great place to do some treetop birding. This viewpoint affords birders the luxury of being able to look down on some species notorious for perching in tall trees. **Band-tailed Pigeons** are almost always present, perched on top of the cedars and hemlocks below you. **Rufous Hummingbirds** (April-June) often perch atop the trees as well, and offer fabulous views of their sparkling colours. In May and June, the trees and shrubs are full of song—**Willow Flycatchers** (June), **Swainson's Thrushes**, **Warbling Vireos**, **MacGillivray's**, **Wilson's**, and **Orange-crowned warblers**, **Black-headed Grosbeaks** and **Western Tanagers** are all possible. **Bald Eagles** often sail by.

As you continue up the road, watch for **Blue Grouse** on the roadsides, especially early in the morning. The deep, hooting calls of the males can be heard anywhere along the road in spring, but become more numerous at higher elevations. The stretch of road near the cross-country ski area is prime **Red-breasted Sapsucker** habitat. They love the thin-barked hemlocks for drilling sap-wells. In May and early June, listen for their drum-rolls, which, like all sapsucker tattoos, start out fast and end very slowly. Later in the summer, their nests can sometimes be found by listening for the incessant begging calls of the young.

At the main downhill ski area parking lot, listen for the musical whistles of **Fox Sparrows** singing on the slopes just above the parking lot (along the start of the Baden-Powell Trail). This is one of the only places in the Vancouver area where this species breeds. A slow circuit of the Yew Lake nature trail on a May or June morning might yield **Blue Grouse** (at least the sound, if not the sight!), **Vaux's Swifts**, **Red-breasted Sapsuckers**, **Olive-sided Flycatchers**, **Gray Jays**, **Steller's Jays**, **Common Ravens**, **Chestnut-backed Chickadees**, **Hermit** and **Varied thrushes**, **Orange-crowned**, **MacGillivray's** and **Wilson's warblers**, **Red Crossbills** and more. Try whistling like a **Northern Pygmy-Owl** here (or anywhere in the Cypress Bowl area); you will at least attract mobbing passerines, if not the diminutive owl itself.

A side trip to the burn area northeast of Yew Lake is often worth taking, especially in August and September, when raptor migration brings **Sharp-shinned**, **Cooper's** and **Red-tailed hawks**, **Northern Harriers**, **American Kestrels** and perhaps other species using the updrafts on the mountain slopes and cutting through the Cypress Creek Valley shortcut to the rest of the North Shore mountain ridges. A longer hike up the Howe Sound Crest Trail could yield more subalpine specialties, notably a **Three-toed Woodpecker**. This is the most consistent site for this species in the Lower Mainland.

Winter and early spring have their charms here, but you will usually have to stick to the roads if you do not want to don your skis or snowshoes to enter the forests. As well, the winter forests are rather silent, except for a few chattering flocks of **Chestnut-backed**

Chickadees and *Golden-crowned Kinglets* or the croak of a *Common Raven* overhead. However, winter is the best time of year to see *Gray Jays*, and a *Northern Pygmy-Owl* or *Red-breasted Sapsucker* may occasionally be seen.

Written by Dick Cannings

Bears and Other Wild Animals

Bears and other creatures, large and small, share our parks and wilderness areas with the birds and the birders. All of these animals should be treated with the utmost respect and consideration. Always give them a comfortable distance and never feed any sort of wild animal. The best way to view wildlife, especially bears, is through your binoculars or, even better, from the safety of your vehicle.

From time to time, depending on seasonal conditions, you may encounter bears in some of the Vancouver-area parks. The most likely locations are parks in the North Shore mountains—Cypress and Mount Seymour provincial parks, Golden Ears Provincial Park and Minnekhada Regional Park—and Burns Bog in Delta.

Encounters with bears could happen at any time, but are more likely in the spring and fall. You might see a bear grazing on the luscious fresh grass on the roadside leading to the mountain parks in the spring, or encounter hungry bears raiding blueberry fields and fruit-producing trees in the fall after a dry summer has left little to eat in wild berry patches. Whatever the case may be, *never* approach the animal; retreat to a safe location, take an alternative route to avoid it, or wait until it has moved well away from the area. If you should happen to come across a bear suddenly on a trail, make some noise, like talking loudly or clapping your hands, and back away slowly—*never* run. The bear will usually do its utmost to avoid you and will leave the area. Many hikers attach bells to their packs to reduce the likelihood of an encounter.

Written by Catherine J. Aitchison

Vancouver Natural History Society
P.O. Box 3021, Vancouver, B.C. V6B 3X5
Events and Information, and **Bird Alert**
Tel: (604) 737-3074, 24 hours a day

Fraser Delta

11. Reifel Migratory Bird Sanctuary and Vicinity

Reifel Migratory Bird Sanctuary is situated at the mouth of the South Arm of the Fraser River, less than an hour's drive from the city of Vancouver. It is 8 km (5 mi) west of Ladner on Westham Island in Delta. The non-profit British Columbia Waterfowl Society maintains and runs the sanctuary and encourages appreciation of wetland wildlife habitat in the Fraser River estuary.

Reifel Migratory Bird Sanctuary is named after George C. Reifel, who purchased the north end of Westham Island in 1927. By 1929 most of the dyking and reclamation work was completed and he built the family home. Initially grain was grown on the farm, but in World War II his son, George H. Reifel, grew much-needed sugar beet seed. On 202 ha (500 a) the farm supplied one-third of the country's demand in 1961.

Largely as a result of the efforts of conservationists Barry Leach and Fred Auger, the B.C. Waterfowl Society was formed. The society leased some land from the Reifels to manage as a bird sanctuary. Ducks Unlimited (Canada) created numerous ponds and islands on some of the dyked land to enhance the area for waterfowl nesting and loafing. The provincial government purchased additional foreshore, bringing the total sanctuary area to 344 ha (850 a). The federal government bought the Reifel farm in 1973, and the B.C. Waterfowl Society now leases this crown land from the Canadian Wildlife Service.

The sanctuary is situated on the Fraser River flood plain. If the area was not dyked, it would flood on every high tide, as would the rest of Westham Island. The sanctuary itself has about 4 km (2.5 mi) of trails, most of which are on dykes that give a little height to see across an otherwise flat area. All the waterways and ponds are controlled to maximize bird use; some areas are dry in summer, flooded slowly for shorebirds in spring and fall, and then completely flooded for ducks and geese in winter. Water comes in at high tide under control and flows out at low tide. This means that much of the water in the sanctuary is brackish. However, the three sloughs on the east side of the sanctuary contain freshwater.

Westham Island is prime agricultural land on which farmers grow a wide variety of crops, including potatoes, corn, grain, cabbage, strawberries and raspberries. The 1-km (.6-mi) driveway into the sanctuary parking lot is bordered by alder and blackberries, with a few coniferous species and Pacific crabapples. The central area has a lot of shrub cover and Douglas-fir and black cottonwood trees. The outer west dyke is more open, with sparse vegetation. An extensive cattail marsh stretches to the west towards the Strait of Georgia. The highest tides in this area reach 4.8 m (16 ft), while the lows go down to 1.2 m (4 ft).

Directions

From Vancouver, take Highway 99 (Oak Street) south. Stay in the right-hand lane when passing through the George Massey Tunnel, ready for the Ladner exit (#29) onto River Road immediately after you come out of the tunnel. This is the "back way" to Ladner, which will take you past the entrance to Ladner Harbour Park (detailed later in this section). Stop here if you wish, or continue west into Ladner, turning left at the stop sign, and right after 3 blocks onto 47A Avenue. After a short time, 47A becomes River Road West. Follow it for 2.9 km (1.8 mi), turning right onto Westham Island Bridge. (There is a Reifel Migratory Bird Sanctuary sign at this corner.) Follow Westham Island Road for 4.8 km (3 mi), until you arrive at two sets of gates. Take the left-hand turn and follow the driveway for 1 km (.6 mi) to the parking lot.

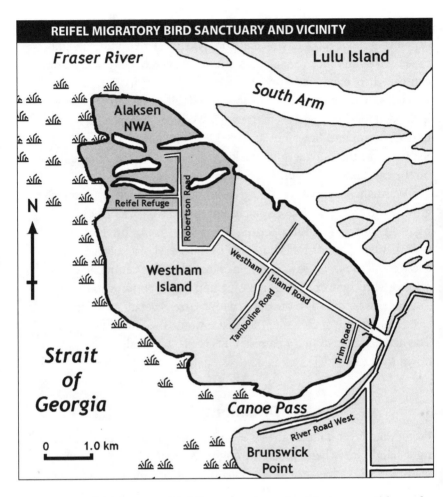

REIFEL MIGRATORY BIRD SANCTUARY AND VICINITY

Fraser River
Lulu Island
South Arm
Alaksen NWA
Reifel Refuge
Robertson Road
Westham Island
Westham Island Road
Tamboline Road
Trim Road
N
Strait of Georgia
Canoe Pass
River Road West
Brunswick Point
0 1.0 km

Reifel Migratory Bird Sanctuary has wheelchair-accessible washrooms, picnic tables, a "warming hut" for cold-weather lunches and a gift shop selling a variety of items from chocolate bars to binoculars. A collection of 250 stuffed birds can be viewed on weekends or by arrangement. Guided tours are offered to pre-booked groups of eight or more people at a reduced admission price. A guided tour is also offered to the public every Sunday morning at 10 A.M. The sanctuary is open every day from 9 A.M. to 4 P.M. (no entry after 4 P.M.). There is a small admission fee, and reduced fees for children and seniors.

Bird Species

A list of birds seen in the sanctuary during the past week is always posted on the gift shop window, and a "Sightings Book" is located at the side of the building. For up-to-the-minute information on particular species and where to find them in the sanctuary, inquire at the gift shop.

The mixed habitats at the sanctuary have supported 272 species of birds. In winter, **waterfowl** and **raptors** are at their best. A flock of 25,000 **Snow Geese** come in by mid-October from Wrangel Island, Siberia; they can be found offshore at low tide and often in the fields at high tide. Many **wintering ducks** and **shorebirds** follow the same pattern of being out in the intertidal areas at low tide and flying in at high tide.

Over 24 **duck species** have been recorded, and three **merganser species** can often be found in winter. **Eurasian Wigeon** can be seen on most days in winter on the sloughs and fields, feeding with the flocks of **American Wigeon**. A few pairs of **Wood Ducks** and **Ring-necked Ducks** may also be seen. In winter, large flocks of **Trumpeter Swans** (high count of 1,400) plus a few **Tundra Swans** feed and roost offshore as well as on Westham Island and the Delta farmland.

In summer, **Cinnamon** and **Blue-winged teal** are attracted to the sanctuary, along with large numbers of **Gadwall**, which, after **Mallards**, are the most common breeding duck. **Northern Pintails**, **American Wigeon** and **Northern Shovelers** also attempt to breed, but in very small numbers. Large flocks of **Canada Geese** moult in the area in July and August, and up to 2,000 can be seen on Westham Island.

Peak migration times at the sanctuary are April, May, and August through October. In April there is an influx of fish-eating birds at the river mouth and offshore feeding on eulachon (an oily, herring-like fish). Up to 2,000 **Pacific Loons** and other loon species gather offshore to feed before moving north to breeding areas. **Red-breasted** and **Common mergansers** also gather here, along with hundreds of **Bald Eagles** and **Double-crested Cormorants**. Many **gulls** are also present, but are quite hard to identify due to their distance offshore.

A total of 41 species of **shorebirds** has been seen at the sanctuary. The first **Western Sandpipers** of the fall start south in late June, followed by **Least** and a few **Semipalmated sandpipers**. Later, in July and August, large numbers of **Greater** and **Lesser yellowlegs**, along with **Long-** and **Short-billed dowitchers** also start to move south. Other shorebird species seen here range from an accidental **Spotted Redshank** to the more regular but uncommon **Ruff** and **Sharp-tailed**, **Baird's** and **Solitary sandpipers**.

Shorebirds are also eager to get north in the spring. **Dunlin**, **Western Sandpipers**, **Black-bellied Plovers** and **dowitchers** pass through in April. Some can be seen resting or feeding in the west field at high tide, offering a closer look at their fresh plumage.

Passerines follow a similar pattern of arrival at the sanctuary. Although warblers, flycatchers and other passerines start a little later, in mid-May, they do not return until August. One of the best areas for passerines is in the northeast corner and along the slough walk just east of the parking lot. The winter **sparrows—White-crowned**, **Golden-crowned**, **Fox** and **Song**—can be found along the east dyke. Lucky observers may occasionally find **Lincoln's**, **Swamp**, **White-throated** and **Harris's sparrows** on any trail, although a traditional spot to find a **Swamp Sparrow** is on the dyke trail near the observation tower.

Black-crowned Night-Herons, birds that are very hard to find in the Vancouver area, have wintered on Fuller's Slough for several recent consecutive years. They often perch in the willows on the sunny side of the slough. **Green Herons** might also be seen in the sanctuary from August to the end of September.

Many birds of prey can be seen at Reifel: **Red-tailed** and **Cooper's hawks**, **Bald Eagles**, **Northern Harriers**, **Great Horned** and **Barn owls** all breed in this area. **Rough-legged Hawks**, **Gyrfalcons** and **Snowy Owls** come down from the north to winter here, while **Peregrine Falcons**, **Merlins**, **Sharp-shinned Hawks** and **Northern Saw-whet Owls** are seen regularly throughout the winter. **Turkey Vultures** and **American Kestrels** are seen as they pass through and rarely stay more than a few days. The first **White-tailed Kite** in Canada was seen here in April 1990.

Ladner Harbour Park

As you travel along River Road towards Ladner, you may want to make a brief stop at Ladner Harbour Park. The turnoff into the park is on the right, approximately 400 m (1/4 mi) past Ferry Road.

A mixture of deciduous woodland with a number of large cottonwoods attracts a broad spectrum of passerines in spring and summer, including **Bewick's Wrens**, **Black-headed Grosbeaks**, **Yellow Warblers**, **Common Yellowthroats** and **Western Tanagers**. It's a good place to view **Cliff**, **Barn**, **Violet-green** and **Tree swallows**. Check the marsh areas for **Virginia Rails**, **Soras**, **Marsh Wrens** and the occasional **Short-eared Owl**. This is generally a reliable area for **Bullock's Orioles**, particularly adjacent to the warden's hut. In May and September, the park attracts numerous migrants, such as **Cassin's**, **Warbling** and **Red-eyed vireos**, **Nashville**, **Townsend's** and **Yellow-rumped warblers** and **Western Tanagers**.

In winter, carefully check flocks of **chickadees** and **kinglets** for an occasional wintering warbler; **Common Yellowthroats**, **Orange-crowned** and **Yellow-rumped warblers** usually turn up here to be included in the Christmas Bird Count. Several **Bald Eagles** often perch in the tall cottonwoods in winter. Unusual species show up from time to time; a **Blue Jay** visited for a short time, and a **Swamp Sparrow** has recently been recorded in this locality in the winter.

Westham Island

After leaving Ladner on River Road West, the series of sharp bends near 3653 River Road West is worth a pause to look for **Mourning Doves**. After turning right onto Westham Island Road and crossing the single-lane wooden bridge (extremely slippery when wet), park safely on the immediate right. Walk back onto the bridge and view Canoe Pass. In the fall and winter, **Red-necked**, **Western** and **Horned grebes**, **Common** and **Barrow's goldeneyes** and various other diving ducks can be seen, and, on rare occasions in late spring, one or two **Mute Swans**.

All of the lands of Westham Island are private property, including the dykes. Please do not trespass. The first turn left is Trim Road, which gives good views over Canoe Pass. At low tide a mudbank is exposed, which, particularly in the winter, holds good numbers of **gull species**. This is a good area to see raptors; along with the more regular **Bald Eagles** and **Red-tailed Hawks**, rarer species, including **Peregrine Falcons**, **Merlins** and **American Kestrels**, may be observed. On extremely rare occasions in the winter, both a **Gyrfalcon** and a **Prairie Falcon** have been seen. In winter, scan the fields from Trim Road, particularly to the extreme northwest, as **Snowy Owls** have been observed here.

Tamboline Road is approximately 1.4 km (.9 mi) farther along Westham Island Road on the left. The ditches may hold **Common Snipe** from fall to spring, and various **dabbling ducks** in spring and summer, including all three species of teal. During **warbler** migration, suitable weather conditions can yield a varied "fall-out" in the many hedges and trees. The reeded dyke .8 km (.5 mi) along the left-hand side at #4380 is a good location to look for overwintering **Lincoln's Sparrows**. Large numbers of **Golden-crowned Sparrows** can be found along this stretch; **White-crowned** and **Fox sparrows** are present during spring migration. The junction of Tamboline Road and Westham Island Road is a good location to watch for **Barn Owls** at dusk. Unusual species, such as **Yellow-headed Blackbirds** or a **Harris's Sparrow**, are sometimes seen in this area.

In fall and winter the fields of Westham Island can be teeming with wildfowl but, due to the pressures of hunting, the birds tend not to be present during the daytime. However, outside the hunting season the views can be spectacular. Peak numbers of **Snow Geese** can exceed 25,000 and **Trumpeter Swans** can number up to 1,400. Many can be observed feeding in farm fields at high tide. The predominant duck species is **American Wigeon**, and high numbers of **Eurasian Wigeon** can also be seen. A high count of 100 male **Eurasian Wigeon** was made in a flock of approximately 3,000 **American Wigeon** in February 1989. Sloughs are worth pausing at; both **Hooded** and **Common mergansers** may be seen here at close quarters.

Written by John Ireland and Robin Owen; revised by John Ireland

Tides

Tide levels are important when looking for water birds and shorebirds. If you do not have a copy of "Canadian Tide and Current Tables," published annually by Fisheries and Oceans Canada (available at marinas and in the reference section of most libraries), check the weather section of Vancouver-area newspapers for daily tide levels and times. The *Vancouver Sun* and the *Vancouver Province* are the two largest daily newspapers. Tide information can also be found on TV and on the Internet (the Weather Channel is #23 in Vancouver; website: www.theweathernetwork.com). Readings for Point Atkinson, the rocky peninsula in West Vancouver on which Lighthouse Park is situated, are used by most local birders.

Tidal fluctuations in waters around Vancouver are large, from as little as .8 m (2.6 ft) to as much as 4.9 m (16.1 ft) within a 24-hour period. Daily high tides vary from about 3.6 m (11.8 ft) to 4.9 m (16 ft).

On a sandy or muddy shoreline, most waterfowl are best seen during moderately high tides of 3.7 m (12 ft) and higher, although Green-winged Teal and sometimes other dabbling ducks often congregate to feed on tidal flats. Shorebirds are generally best seen during tides of about 3 m (10 ft) to 3.8 m (12.5 ft). During lower tides there is so much exposed mud and sand that shorebirds range over an enormous area. High tides push them nearer shore, where they can be seen more easily. On the other hand, maximum tides of 4.6 m (15 ft) or more force shorebirds to other areas that may be inaccessible to birders. Plan to arrive at *least* 1 hour (2 hours may be better) before the expected optimum viewing time; the water moves in surprisingly fast.

Tides are also important when viewing shorebirds and waterfowl along a rocky coastline. At low tide, exposed or shallow beds of mussels and barnacles may attract sea ducks, turnstones, oystercatchers, gulls and other birds to the area.

Birding locations described in this book that are particularly tide-sensitive include Boundary Bay (north side), Blackie Spit, Roberts Bank, Iona Beach Regional Park and Iona South Jetty, Boundary Bay Regional Park and the Compensation Lagoon at the Tsawwassen Ferry Terminal.

Optimum tides for viewing shorebirds are: Roberts Bank, 3.7 m (12 ft); base of Iona jetty, 3.5 m to 3.7 m (11.5 to 12 ft); 12th Avenue Lagoon at Boundary Bay Regional Park, 3.8 m and flooding to 4 m (12.5 ft to 13 ft); northern Boundary Bay between 88th and 96th Streets, 4 m (13 ft). In front of "the Mansion," where there is a deep channel, birding is good even on a low tide.

Written by Catherine J. Aitchison from information provided by Hue MacKenzie, Richard Swanston and Brian Self

12. Roberts Bank/Tsawwassen Ferry Terminal/Brunswick Point

The Roberts Bank Superport jetty was built in the late 1960s. It is 5 km (3.1 mi) long, with a bulk coal loading facility and a new container port. The coal port, the largest bulk loading terminal on the west coast of North America, is operated by Westshore Terminals Ltd. and ships coal to such Pacific Rim countries as Japan, Korea and Taiwan. The coal is brought by unit trains from southeastern British Columbia and Alberta. Containers are primarily from the Pacific Rim, destined for the North American market, with some shipped on to the East Coast and then to Europe.

This was once a sleepy, birdwatcher-friendly place with two or three rail lines running the length of the causeway. The Deltaport Container Terminal, begun in 1992, brought an addition to the rail lines (which now number eight) and a great increase in large, fast-moving truck traffic on the narrow, two-lane roadway. With the new maze of dangerous tracks carrying electronically operated trains, rail company police and security officers now enforce the No Trespassing signs prohibiting crossing to the west side of the terminal over the tracks by car or foot. On the south side of the causeway there is a dirt road, which runs parallel to the main road. This is the birder's best access to shoreline and mud flat views. In the future, car access may not be possible, although it should still be possible to walk along the shoreline.

Access on foot north across the tracks to the dyke trail, which runs north to Brunswick Point, is still permitted, but it can be blocked by trains for as long as 1/2 hour. As it is very dangerous to cross between cars, you may have to wait or walk around the stopped train, which could be up to 1.6 km (1 mi) long! *Do not attempt to cross through a stopped train.* They can move without warning. Be careful to obey all the No Trespassing signs in this area.

The Tsawwassen Ferry Terminal and causeway were built in

the mid-sixties. Ferries sail from this port to Swartz Bay (for Victoria), Nanaimo (Duke Point) and destinations on the Gulf Islands. When the terminal was expanded about 10 years ago, a "Habitat Compensation Area" was built with the goal of replacing valuable fish habitat. This area has come to be known by local birders as the Compensation Lagoon. It provides very good high-tide roosting for many **shorebirds**, **terns** and **gulls**.

The point of land immediately south of Canoe Pass and south of Westham Island is known to Vancouver birders by the unofficial name of Brunswick Point. It is an easy walk (about 1 1/2 hours) along the dyke from Brunswick Point to Roberts Bank, with good birding along the way.

The western side of this area is formed by the Strait of Georgia. Roberts Bank itself forms part of the deltaic deposits of the Fraser River, while Brunswick Point contains an extensive cattail marsh. The farmlands above the high-tide level are protected by a system of dykes. Potatoes and other mixed vegetables and cereals are grown in the fields, which are surrounded by drainage ditches and, in some places, by hedgerows.

Roberts Bank
Directions

To reach Roberts Bank from downtown Vancouver, take Highway 99 (Oak Street) south, following signs for B.C. Ferries to Victoria. Take exit #28 to Highway 17 south, heading towards Tsawwassen. Proceed south on Highway 17 for approximately 5 km (3.1 mi), passing through the intersection of Highway 10, until you see a sign on the right that directs you to Deltaport Way. This new highway takes you through farmland directly to the Deltaport/Roberts Bank jetty. The overpass near the end of the road provides a gorgeous view towards Brunswick Point and Vancouver Island. *Do not stop* on the roadside or the overpass. The container traffic is fast-moving and dangerous. Watch for the gravel road that parallels the causeway on your left and any entrances that are still available. There are

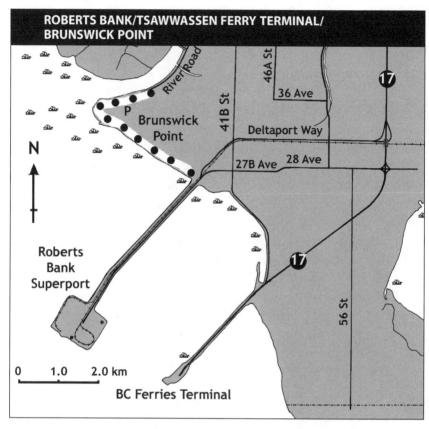

ROBERTS BANK/TSAWWASSEN FERRY TERMINAL/ BRUNSWICK POINT

Brunswick Point

River Road

46A St

36 Ave

41B St

Deltaport Way

27B Ave 28 Ave

N

Roberts Bank Superport

56 St

0 1.0 2.0 km

BC Ferries Terminal

also some small blacktop parking areas to the left. They may by now be marked No Parking, in which case return to the overpass, park underneath it and walk back along the gravel road.

Bird Species

In the area between the Roberts Bank jetty and the Tsawwassen Ferry Terminal, the level of the tide has a considerable influence on the distribution of the birds. At low tide, *shorebirds* and *herons* feed on the mud flats, which extend most of the way out along the jetty. When the tide comes up, the mud flats disappear and the shorebirds are replaced by *ducks* and *loons*. Depending on the species you are hoping to find, possibly the best birding in this area is on a rising tide. A 3.4- to 3.7-m (11- or 12-ft) high tide is the best for bringing *shorebirds* close to shore, but not so far as to scatter them into the fields.

Winter is the season when the most birds are normally present. *Common Loons* live up to their name; very rarely, a *Yellow-billed Loon* can be found. *Horned Grebes* are common and there may be an occasional *Eared Grebe*. Waterfowl are abundant; large flocks of *Northern Pintails* and *American Wigeon* may have as many as 20 drake *Eurasian Wigeon* scattered among them. (We will leave the count of the females for very experienced birders.) All three species of scoters can be found; *Surf Scoters* are the most numerous. Good numbers of *Greater Scaup* are often present. Several hundred *Black-bellied Plovers* frequent the mud flats in winter, along with large flocks of *Dunlin*. If you search carefully through these winter flocks, you may be able to find an occasional *Western Sandpiper*. *Bald Eagles* commonly perch on the tall hydro poles and make excellent subjects for photographers.

In spring, large flocks of *Brant* may cover the water as they feed on eelgrass. Smaller numbers of Brant may be found fairly regularly from late November to early April. Many *shorebirds*, including *Western*, *Least* and *Baird's sandpipers*, can be found during both spring and fall migrations. The shorebirds are often harassed by *Peregrine Falcons* and *Merlins*.

In early summer, the waters are generally fairly empty, but large flocks of *Great Blue Herons* feed on the tidal flats. On May 23, 1992, 400 of these birds were counted feeding here. This is the greatest number of this species reported feeding at a single location in the Vancouver area. These herons come from the large heronry at Point Roberts, Washington.

The waters on the north side of the Roberts Bank jetty have essentially the same bird species as the south side.

For several years, the hydro substation and power pylons at the base of the Roberts Bank jetty have been favourite winter perches of a *Gyrfalcon*. A *Prairie Falcon* has also frequented this area in recent winters. In season, it is possible to observe all five species of falcons in a single day in this general area. Occasionally a **Cattle Egret** can be found in the winter, feeding among cattle or horses on the nearby farms. The hedgerows along the dyke in this area can yield five or more species of **sparrows—House**, **Song**, **White-crowned**, **Golden-crowned** and **Lincoln's**—and other small passerines. At high tide, the fields contain roosting **shorebirds** and accompanying **raptors**.

Tsawwassen Ferry Terminal
Directions

To reach the ferry terminal, follow the directions above for Roberts Bank, but *do not turn off Highway 17*, which takes you directly to the terminal. Highway signage is very clear all along this route. Look for a new small parking area to the right as you approach the widening of the traffic lanes nearing the ticketing area. This is called Windsurfers' Corner. It is possible to park here *very briefly* and quickly scope the area between the two causeways, but windsurfers have a prior claim to this parking. A much better idea is to park in the short-term pay parking area near the terminal entrance (the passenger drop-off area), then walk back through the main parking lot and cross the road. Be extremely careful of the traffic! From here you can view the Compensation Lagoon, which consists of an artificial salt marsh created to compensate for habitat lost to terminal expansion. This location has proved to be very attractive to certain species, especially **shorebirds**. *Do not* walk out onto the berms or the marsh. For bus access to the terminal, see page 193.

Bird Species

Jaegers and **terns** are common offshore in late summer, and numerous **cormorants** roost on the rocky breakwater. (A gravel road runs along the south side of the jetty, but in future it may not be accessible by car. As you approach the jetty, look for an access point near the base of the jetty, to your left, or park safely and walk.) Sometimes **Snow Buntings** can be seen along this road from

November to March. Search the rocky shoreline for **Black Oystercatchers**, **Black Turnstones**, **Surfbirds** and even a **Rock Sandpiper**, which comes as a winter visitor.

Birding at the Compensation Lagoon is very tide-dependent, being best on a rising or low high tide. Although this marsh area is fairly new, it is gaining a reputation as a good place to see **shorebirds** at migration time, and even to find some rarities. It seems to be particularly attractive to the larger, longer-legged shorebirds, such as **Black-bellied Plovers**, and **Willet** and **Marbled Godwit** have both been observed. **Black Oystercatchers** breed here, and in summer there can be hundreds of non-breeding **Caspian Terns** loafing in the area. Both **Ruddy** and **Black turnstones** are also seen. Check the flocks of **Bonaparte's Gulls** for more unusual species.

Note: For information about birding from the ferries themselves, see "Birding from B.C. Ferries," page 191.

Brunswick Point
Directions

To reach Brunswick Point, follow the directions to Reifel Migratory Bird Sanctuary, but do not turn right onto Westham Island. Instead, follow River Road West to the end, where you can park on the roadside and walk along the dyke. Please respect the parking signs and keep farm gateways clear. It is about a 1 1/2-hour easy walk on the dyke from Brunswick Point to Roberts Bank. You will have salt marsh, farmland and open water to search for birds. Alternatively, you can park under the overpass at Roberts Bank, carefully cross the railway tracks and walk the other way (see Roberts Bank directions).

Brunswick Point can also be reached by car from Roberts Bank by turning north off Deltaport Way onto 41B Street. This takes you to River Road West at a point just west of Ladner village. Turn left (west) at the T-junction of 41B and River Road West to reach Reifel Migratory Bird Sanctuary or Brunswick Point. Consult a current map for clarity.

Bird Species

This is an excellent birding spot from at least September through May, when large numbers of waterfowl are present. The main attractions are **swans** and **Snow Geese**. Up to 400 swans, mainly **Trumpeters**, concentrate here and at Reifel Migratory Bird Sanctuary from November to March; up to 10,000 **Snow Geese** can be seen from October to April, although the geese are much less predictable. Since the late 1980s, most of the swans feed on Westham Island during the day, but they return to Brunswick Point in impressive flights to roost for the night. Thousands of **dabbling ducks**, often including several **Eurasian Wigeon**, feed in the marshes and mud flats around the point. The waterfowl can be better seen at high tide, when they are forced closer to the dyke. Flocks of up to 10,000 **Dunlin** can be seen feeding on the flats or flying by in dense masses. Canoe Pass, the arm of the Fraser River between Brunswick Point and Westham Island to the north, usually has rather few birds, but **Western Grebes**, **Double-crested Cormorants**, **Buffleheads** and **Common** and **Red-breasted mergansers** may be seen.

The farm fields inside the dyke are excellent for birds of prey, including many **Red-tailed** and **Rough-legged hawks**, **Northern Harriers** and **Bald Eagles**. **Peregrine Falcons** and **Merlins** are often seen and, in some winters, a **Gyrfalcon** or **Prairie Falcon** may be present. Scan the fields and treetops often as you walk along the dyke.

Some of the most interesting birds can be found in the shrubs and dense weed patches just outside the dyke. This is a regular spot in winter for **American Tree Sparrows**, and there are several records of **Swamp Sparrows**, also in winter. A **Short-eared Owl** may burst out of the shrubbery, and, in an irruption year, it's possible to see **Snowy Owls** along the dyke or perching on a log out in the marsh. **Marsh Wrens** are resident but most easily found in spring and summer, when they are very vocal on territory. Occasionally, you will be rewarded with the sight of an **American Bittern** flying low over the marsh.

The Brunswick Point area can produce some interesting birds

during spring and fall migration. Especially worth checking are the shrubby thickets and tall poplars near the west end of West River Road. The brush can hide a variety of sparrows and warblers, including **Lincoln's Sparrows** and even a rare **White-throated Sparrow**. Occasionally a **Long-eared Owl** or **Barn Owl** conceals itself in the densest brush. **Horned Larks**, **Lapland Longspurs** and **Snow Buntings** are sometimes seen along the dyke in early spring or late fall. Spectacular concentrations of **Western Sandpipers**, with smaller numbers of other shorebirds, can be seen on the point in spring and fall (especially in the last week of April), and small flocks of the locally rare **Greater White-fronted Geese** occasionally stop on the point in late April or early May.

Possibly the nicest time to visit Brunswick Point is on an evening in late April or early May, on a rising tide just before sunset. Sit on a log, watch the sunset over the Strait of Georgia and listen for the booming of an **American Bittern** or the calls of **Soras** and **Virginia Rails**.

Written by Gerry Ansell; revised by Richard Swanston and Catherine J. Aitchison, with additional information from Brian Self

13. Point Roberts, Washington

Point Roberts, Washington, although in the United States, is nonetheless included in the Vancouver Checklist Area and is a favourite location among Vancouver birders for seabird watching. The area consists of the tip of a peninsula, which stretches southwards at the west end of Boundary Bay. The northern portion of the peninsula contains the municipality of Tsawwassen; the southern portion, below the international boundary of the 49th parallel, is the community of Point Roberts. The area has the look and feel of a seaside resort community, with much of the oceanfront property built up with permanent or seasonal residences. However, there is still plenty of accessible beach, and the high bluffs at Lily Point provide good vantage points for scanning the ocean and western Boundary Bay. Lighthouse Marine Park, on the western tip of the peninsula, provides some of the best seabird watching in the Vancouver area, as it protrudes into fairly open ocean. Seabirds tend to fly "around the corner" here, in and out of Boundary Bay, and a seawatch with a scope in a fairly protected spot can be extremely worthwhile in fall and winter. There is also plenty of good woodland birding, making a trip to Point Roberts doubly rewarding.

Directions

To reach Point Roberts from downtown Vancouver, take Highway 99 (Oak Street) south and take the Highway 17 exit (#28) heading towards Tsawwassen. At the second set of lights (56th Street), turn left (south) and continue until you reach the international boundary. The U.S. side is Point Roberts. *Please note that overseas visitors require a visa to enter the United States.*

Once you cross the international boundary, you will be southbound on Tyee Drive. Continue south for approximately 3.5 km (2.2 mi) to A.P.A. Road. Turn left (east) and continue for 2.5 km (1.6 mi) until you see a cemetery on your right. In front of you will be a gate and a path that leads to Lily Point. At the time of writing, birders can park along the road next to the cemetery, but this will likely change, as a proposal to turn Lily Point into a golf course has recently been approved. Contacting those people listed at the end of the VNHS Vancouver Bird Alert (see page 14) is likely the best way to find out how to gain access to the point in future.

Bird Species

To your left when you park is a large clearing overgrown with alder, blackberry and other shrubs bordered by second-growth deciduous forest. Especially during migration, many songbirds can be seen or heard along the perimeter of the clearing or all along the trail down

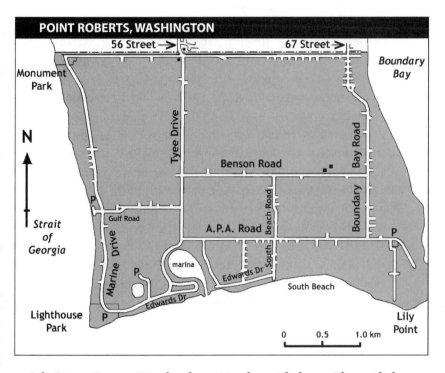

POINT ROBERTS, WASHINGTON

56 Street → 67 Street →

Boundary Bay

Monument Park

N

Tyee Drive

Benson Road

Boundary Bay Road

Strait of Georgia

Gulf Road

A.P.A. Road

Beach Road

Boundary

P

Marine Drive

marina

Edwards Dr

South Beach Road

P

South Beach

Edwards Dr

Lighthouse Park

P

Lily Point

0   0.5   1.0 km

to Lily Point. *Downy Woodpeckers*, *Northern Flickers*, *Olive-sided Flycatchers*, *Black-capped* and *Chestnut-backed chickadees*, *Bewick's* and *Winter wrens*, *kinglets*, *vireos*, *warblers*, *Black-headed Grosbeaks*, *sparrows* and *finches* are seen in appropriate seasons. This is a very good location for *Hutton's Vireos* all year, but mainly from February through May, when they are singing on territory. At other times of year watch for them in mixed-species flocks with chickadees or kinglets. These birds respond well to "pishing," so be sure to try this. Scan the skies for *Red-tailed*, *Sharp-shinned* and *Cooper's hawks*, especially during migration. *Barred* and *Great Horned owls* and *Western Screech-Owls* have all been recorded from this end of A.P.A. Road.

A gravel road leads from the gate to Lily Point. The cliffs overlooking Boundary Bay provide an excellent vantage point for scoping for *alcids*, *grebes* (especially during fall moult), *loons*, *Barrow's Goldeneyes*, *Harlequin Ducks*, *scoters* and other seabirds. With some luck, you may see **Pileated Woodpeckers** and **Red-breasted Nuthatches** in these mature woods from the paved road that turns south just before the cemetery. This road is very good for **songbirds** all year round but, like most areas, can be quiet during winter. Listen for **Red Crossbills** and **Pine Siskins** flying overhead.

Drive back towards Tyee Drive along A.P.A. Road, turning right onto Boundary Bay Road at the stop sign. Turn left onto Benson Road and continue until you reach the Point Roberts Volunteer Fire Department parking lot on your right. Park in the parking lot and walk back towards the east where there is an access road to the primary school and a trail that leads into the Baker Community Field. The birds that can be seen here are similar to those found at A.P.A. Road. A small trail begins at the far end of the field and eventually loops back towards the parking lot. This trail can be very productive for **warblers** and **flycatchers** in spring and summer. Watch overhead for **raptors**.

Continue west along Benson Road until you arrive at South Beach Road on your left. Take this left and proceed down the hill until the road ends at the beach. Scanning this extensive view of the Strait of Georgia may produce good numbers of **sea ducks** during the winter months. Returning to the road, turn west along Edwards Drive instead of heading back up South Beach Road. After approximately .5 km (.3 mi), you will arrive at an open field at the corner of Largaud Drive and Edwards. Park off to the side of the road and scan this field and check the trees across the field for roosting **raptors**. Depending upon the time of year, many species of raptors frequent this field and woodlot. This is one of the best locations in Point Roberts to see **Barn Owls** coursing the field edges at dusk. While parked here, take a brief walk down the gravel lane that leads to the beach. Scanning the beach from here is likely to produce **Sanderling** and **Black Turnstones** in winter. During the summer, be sure to check the open water for possible passing orca (killer whale) pods.

Continue driving west along Edwards Drive for a short distance until you travel through a series of short bends in the road. Pull over and park on the roadside once you arrive at the marina playing field. A walk to the beach will give you a good view of the marina break-water, an excellent area for **Heermann's Gulls**, **Surfbirds** and **Black Turnstones**. **Harlequin Ducks** often haul up in good numbers onto the rocky beach along the marina channel at low tide.

Continue driving up the road (Simundson Drive) until you return to A.P.A. Road. Keep an eye skyward in September and October along the northern horizon for kettles of **Turkey Vultures** and the many other species of migrating raptors. Turn left onto A.P.A. Road and continue until you reach Tyee Drive. Bear left on Tyee and continue through a series of bends until you reach Ocean View Court on your right. This cul-de-sac will give you an excellent view of a pond where **scaup**, **Canvasbacks**, **goldeneyes** and **Buffleheads** are found from October to April. The flocks of **Glaucous-winged** and **Mew gulls** should be checked for possible **Thayer's** and **California gulls**.

Surrounding this future residential subdivision are weedy fields bordered by blackberry hedgerows. By walking along the hedgerows and "pishing" or "squeaking" (October to April), you can find **Spotted Towhees** and **Fox**, **Song**, **Golden-crowned**, **White-crowned** and occasionally **Lincoln's sparrows** (frequent during migration). The weedy fields have **American Goldfinches**, **House Finches** and **Savannah Sparrows** (rare in winter). In the wetter areas you can find **Common Yellowthroats** (spring and summer) and **Common Snipe**. **Northern Shrikes** (winter) and **raptors** occasionally frequent this area. **American Pipits** (in migration) occasionally occur where weeds have managed to take a foothold in the gravel along the edges of the pond, ditches and road. Much more unusual are **Lapland Longspurs** and **Snow Buntings**.

Return to the entrance of this road and turn right along Edwards Drive for another 1 km (.6 mi) towards Lighthouse Marine Park, an excellent location to view seabirds. On your right is a small camp-ground surrounded by pines. During migration these pines can attract songbirds, including an occasional **Mountain Chickadee** (fall). Drive into the park on your left and go to the parking area by the beach. Be sure to bring some U.S. money for the parking fee.

Although many birds frequent the shoreline, this area is best birded by doing a stationary seawatch using a spotting scope. A path running south along the shoreline takes you to the point itself and the small light tower, which is a good spot to set up your scope. The summer months are very quiet here, with only an occasional **Common Loon**, **Surf** or **White-winged scoter** or perhaps another summering **sea duck**. A feeding **Pigeon Guillemot**, **Marbled Murrelet** or **Rhinoceros Auklet** (there is a breeding colony near Sequim, Washington) might also be seen. However, summer is the best time to see orcas; a pod often swims by in the late afternoon, so watch for spouts. Point Roberts is also the best location in the Vancouver area to see grey whales, which move through from March to May. They are sometimes seen from Lily Point, but more often from Lighthouse Marine Park. Other cetaceans seen here include Dall's porpoise, minke whale and false killer whale, but you would be very lucky indeed to spot one of these.

By the end of August things are quite different. **Common Terns** and **Parasitic Jaegers** arrive in the middle of August and are present until the end of October. (The terns arrive and leave earlier than the jaegers.) **Parasitic Jaegers** are often seen harassing **Bonaparte's** or **California gulls**. California Gulls begin to arrive in late July (mostly offshore), but they are gone by the end of October except for the occasional straggler. Bonaparte's Gulls arrive and leave at approximately the same time, but occasionally stragglers remain into winter. Both **Arctic Terns** and **Pomarine Jaegers** are very rare here. **Little Gulls**, **Sabine's Gulls** and **Black-legged Kittiwakes** are seen very occasionally. From late September until early November check the gulls roosting on the pylons for **Heermann's Gulls**. **Common Murres** begin to arrive at this time as well, increasing in numbers throughout the winter. By the first week of May both of these species are difficult to find.

Pelagic and **Double-crested cormorants** occur all year round, while **Brandt's Cormorants** occur from September to April.

Common, *Pacific* and *Red-throated loons* and *Western*, *Red-necked* and *Horned grebes* begin arriving in early September but do not occur in larger numbers until the beginning of October. *Eared Grebes* are rare at this location. (White Rock pier is a much more reliable location.) *Yellow-billed Loons* are also very rare, but worth looking for.

Shorebirds that can be seen along the beach during low tide include *Dunlin*, *Black-bellied Plovers*, *Sanderling* and *Black Turnstones*. Occasionally, from mid-August to October, flocks of *Red-necked Phalaropes* are seen resting off the point or flying past.

From mid-October to late February, sea ducks can be found in large numbers: *Brant*, *Greater Scaup*, *Long-tailed Ducks*, *Black*, *Surf* and *White-winged scoters*, *Common* and *Barrow's goldeneyes*, *Buffleheads*, *Harlequin Ducks* and *Red-breasted Mergansers*. Also seen flying overhead, usually in the early morning, are *Snow Geese* and *Trumpeter Swans*.

From late November to late February keep a sharp lookout for an *Ancient Murrelet*. This is the most reliable place to see this bird in the Vancouver Checklist Area. In September, be sure also to scan the skies for *Turkey Vultures*, which can sometimes be seen migrating south in small flocks.

From Lighthouse Marine Park, turn left onto Edwards Drive, which becomes Marine Drive as it swings north. Follow it for approximately 2 km (1.2 mi) to Gulf Road on the left. Here, at The Breakers Pub parking lot, scan for seabirds and check the *cormorants* and *gulls* roosting on the pylons.

Point Roberts regularly produces rarities of various kinds, especially in winter. Species that have turned up at least once include *Sooty* and *Short-tailed shearwaters*, *Brown Pelican*, *King Eider*, *Red Phalarope*, *Long-tailed Jaeger*, *Little Gull*, *Sabine's Gull*, *Black-legged Kittiwake* and *Cassin's Auklet*. These species are among the most difficult to record with any degree of regularity and should be considered accidental or casual.

Written by Thomas Plath; revised by Ken Klimko and Kyle Elliott

14. Boundary Bay Regional Park
(formerly Beach Grove and Centennial Park)

This small area borders the western perimeter of Boundary Bay. Because of the historical development of the area, combining agriculture, early settlers' cabins and, more recently, rural development, there is an interesting diversity of habitat. It is possible for new birders to observe many species of birds at relatively close range, and the experienced birder has an opportunity to chase down some rare species. The communities of Beach Grove and Centennial Beach still retain many of the old coniferous and deciduous trees combined with native brush and garden habitat. During the spring and fall migrations and the entire winter season, a walk along some of the older side streets will produce most of the west coast *sparrows*, *warblers*, *finches* and other common land birds.

Beach Grove Park and adjacent woodlots create an active all-season corner worthy of a little time, with **Barn, Great Horned** and **Western Screech-Owls** nesting there on a regular basis. The old black cottonwood stand adjacent to the beach is also a winter resting place and roost for at least 25 **Bald Eagles**. The short drive south from the foot of 12th Avenue to the community of Centennial Beach passes through farmland with some good hedges and brushy stands of trees. The road is narrow, with limited parking, but there are plans to upgrade it in the future, allowing safer pull-off areas to view the flooded fields and scan the fence posts in winter.

The dyke walk from the foot of 12th Avenue, with good parking facilities, is the main attraction for local birders. This 1- to 3-km (.6- to 1.8-mi) walk begins in a treed and grassy area, opening up in only 50 m (164 ft) to a shallow intertidal lagoon (12th Avenue Lagoon) on the left and rough grass farmland on the right, interspersed with drainage ditches and small stands of alder and birch trees. The open bay with its huge expanse of intertidal mud flats and sandbars supports good eelgrass meadows that are so critical to winter **Brant** as well as the spring herring spawn and its associated feeding birds. Birding along the shoreline and the bay is dependent on tidal conditions (see "Tides," page 71). Inside the dyke the habitat quickly becomes a combination of old grasses and marshes. It eventually opens up at its southern extremity into an interesting savannah marsh habitat divided into mini-ecosystems by the old sand berms running parallel to the foreshore. Trails criss-cross this habitat, making it easy to search for birds.

At the southern end of this area, Centennial Beach abuts the border with the United States at Point Roberts. The intertidal beaches with their ever-changing sandbars on a receding tide make an ideal resting and preening area for many shorebirds and gulls during the spring and fall migrations, always with the possibility of something unusual dropping in from the nearby open waters off Point Roberts.

Directions

To reach Beach Grove from downtown Vancouver, take Highway 99 (Oak Street) south and take the Highway 17 exit (#28) heading towards Tsawwassen. Turn left at the lights onto 56th Street (Point Roberts turnoff), then turn left at 16th Avenue, driving the 1 km (.6 mi) to Beach Grove Road, where another left turn will lead to Beach Grove Park and the school. Park in the small parking lot (which belongs to the local park) and walk along some of the old back streets and through the Beach Grove Park woodlot area.

To drive directly to the 12th Avenue dyke walk and 12th Avenue Lagoon, continue on 56th Street to 12th Avenue and turn left at the traffic lights. Follow 12th for .7 km (.4 mi), past the golf course to the small parking lot at the foot of 12th Avenue.

To reach the farmland and Centennial Beach, turn right on Boundary Bay Road at the foot of 12th Avenue and continue for 3 km (1.8 mi) to a T-junction. Turn left and follow Centennial Parkway to a parking lot from which you can walk to the beach or the open savannah habitat to the north. It is possible to walk along the beach, the dyke or the trails inside the dyke between the two parking lots at 12th Avenue and Centennial Beach. There are also several public paths to the shoreline between the houses of Beach Grove and Centennial Beach communities.

It is about a 1-hour bus ride from downtown Vancouver to the community of Tsawwassen and Boundary Bay Regional Park. Take the #601 South Delta bus from the corner of Burrard and Dunsmuir streets or the corner of Howe and Georgia streets and get off at 56th

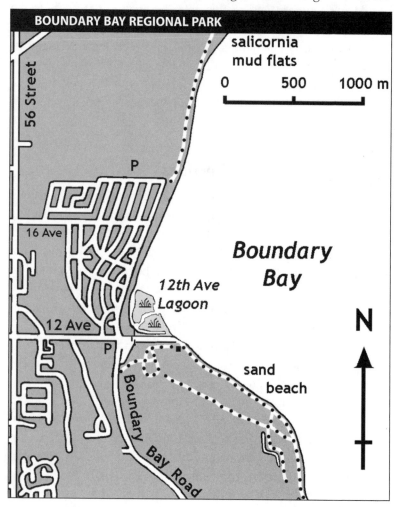

BOUNDARY BAY REGIONAL PARK

56 Street

salicornia mud flats

0   500   1000 m

P

16 Ave

12th Ave Lagoon

Boundary Bay

12 Ave

P

Boundary Bay Road

sand beach

N

Street and 16th Avenue or 12th Avenue in Tsawwassen. Walk a few blocks east to the park.

Approximately one-third of the total area between Boundary Bay Road and the beach is a Greater Vancouver Regional District park, which includes the dyke and beach. Viewing platforms have been built at the lagoon and in several other places. Future plans include the development of a multi-use wildlife habitat with freshwater ponds and marshes taking in all the land east of the road.

Bird Species

Over 210 species of birds have been recorded in this relatively small area. Walking along the dyke has the advantage of permitting close observation of many ducks, gulls, shorebirds and some pelagic species under ideal conditions. The high tide brings the water right up to the dyke and slowly fills the lagoon on the left. Winter populations of **ducks** in the bay exceed 70,000, with up to 18 species of mixed dabbling and diving ducks. Other winter residents include 50,000 **Dunlin** and several hundred **Sanderling**. Add four **loon** species, five **grebes**, three **cormorants** and at least six **gull species** and a winter dyke walk can be exciting.

Among the ducks and pelagic species arriving in early September and resident into April and May, the highlights to be looked for are *Yellow-billed Loon*, *Clark's* and *Eared grebes*, *Tufted Ducks* and high numbers of *Eurasian Wigeon* (up to 23 individuals have been counted from this location).

This is a favoured preening area and resting beach for *Brant*, although very few winter in the bay. The wintering counts are improving, with in excess of 200 birds seen at this location in late winter. Watch for the subspecies *Gray-bellied Brant* among the flocks. The tidal effects on the bay create ideal feeding conditions for the non-migratory *Great Blue Heron* population, and recent fall and winter counts from the 12th Avenue dyke have reached 235 birds. *Bald Eagles* winter locally and scavenge the tide lines of the bay, feeding mainly on ducks and other water birds. Some 68 individuals have been seen here at one time, perched on drift logs or just standing on the beach, sometimes in small groups.

Over 20 raptor species are known to use the bay area, primarily over the winter. The dyke walk at 12th Avenue passes through typical raptor habitat and is a good location to observe **Peregrine Falcons** and **Merlins** as they hunt over the saltwater and fields. A **Prairie Falcon**, **Gyrfalcon** or **Northern Goshawk** may also appear as a rare winter bird. An early-morning or late-evening walk may bring the most success in locating **Barn Owls**, which probably come from the nesting location at Beach Grove Park.

An occasional **Western Sandpiper** or a more unusual wintering **Least Sandpiper** might be found with the wintering flocks of **Dunlin** moving with the tide along this beach. The fall shorebird migration becomes apparent as early as the first week of July, when adult **Western Sandpipers** begin to appear in the lagoon. In some years there is literally no clear break between the spring and fall shorebird migrations in this area. July, August and September are the active months for fall migrants, with the numbers peaking in late August. Over the years, 50 shorebird species have been identified around the bay. The Beach Grove area should, therefore, produce up to 25 species annually. This gives observers the opportunity to study this rather difficult group of birds from relatively close range, as they do not all follow the tide line each day. A few individuals usually remain resting and feeding in the small pools below the dyke.

Western and **Least sandpipers** are the most common shorebirds, but all three **phalaropes** and three species of **plovers** have been seen inside the lagoon. **Greater** and **Lesser yellowlegs**, **dowitchers** and **Killdeer** make up the species of larger shorebirds commonly seen during fall migration, but an occasional **Stilt Sandpiper**, **Ruff** or **Hudsonian Godwit** might also be seen. Spring shorebird migration, from early April until mid-May, may not be as spectacular, but most of the same species of birds can be seen in their more colourful breeding plumages.

The shallow lagoon and the long sloping shoreline outside the sandbar, seen from the viewing platform, are excellent resting and preening areas for up to nine species of **gulls** throughout the year. Several *Franklin's Gulls* may be present during August and September. Up to 30 **Caspian Terns**, including some very young birds, have been seen since 1987 and are a new breeding tern species for the province. These terns are also regular summer residents in this location. A few **Common Terns** pass through as spring migrants, and flocks of up to 150 may be seen in September, either feeding or resting on the shoreline.

Inside the dyke the summer birding is quiet, with the predominant birds being *Savannah Sparrows*. *Cinnamon Teal*, *Mallards*, *Gadwall* and *Blue-winged Teal* all nest here, and single pairs of *Northern Harriers* and *Cooper's Hawks* nest regularly. The marsh is home to a good population of **Marsh Wrens** and a few *Common Yellowthroats*, *Red-winged Blackbirds* and a possible *Sora*. Winter birders should look for an occasional **Swamp Sparrow** and small flocks of **Western Meadowlarks**.

Beach Grove Park seems to have good peak days during spring and fall migrations in May and September, when relatively large numbers of insectivorous species may bunch up in this isolated woodlot. Species that may be found include **Lincoln's Sparrows** and a good representation of **warblers**, with occasional **kingbirds** and *Bullock's Orioles*.

There are eleven months of excellent birding opportunities in the Boundary Bay area; June is the month of least activity.

Written by Allen Poynter; revised by Catherine J. Aitchison

Vancouver Natural History Society
P.O. Box 3021, Vancouver, B.C. V6B 3X5
Events and Information, and **Bird Alert**
Tel: (604) 737-3074, 24 hours a day

15. Boundary Bay—64th Street to 112th Street

Boundary Bay and the many birding sites within this region offer some of the best shorebirding in western Canada. At least 47 species of shorebirds, over 30 of them occurring regularly, have been seen in and around Boundary Bay over the years. It also contains much of Canada's best wintering raptor habitat (all five North American falcons have been found here), large standing gull roosts and huge numbers of wintering waterfowl and other water birds. Its numerous hedgerows, woodlots, sloughs and fallow fields shelter and feed many migrant, wintering and resident passerine species. At least 75 percent of the species on the Vancouver Area Checklist, many of them vagrants, have been seen in the Boundary Bay area.

Boundary Bay is a large, shallow tidal bay, about 16 km (9.9 mi) wide from east to west, and bordered by a dyke along its entire

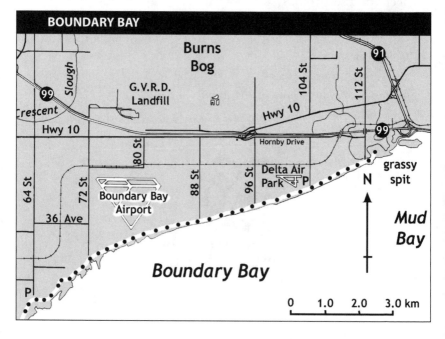

length. The dyke is open to public access, except for the eastern-most segment between the Serpentine and Nicomekl estuaries. At low tide the sand and mud flats extend up to 2 km (1.2 mi) south of the dyke, opening large feeding and roosting areas for waterfowl, gulls and shorebirds. The remnant salt marsh forms a fringe between the high-water mark and the dyke. There are fairly extensive eelgrass beds at several locations offshore. As a general birding destination, Boundary Bay offers many excellent birding locations, from Blackie Spit at the eastern end of the Bay to the 12th Avenue Lagoon and Boundary Bay Regional Park in the west. These latter sites are treated separately elsewhere in this guide (see pages 104 and 86), and this section focuses on the northern segment of Boundary Bay.

The entire length of the bay has been dyked to prevent high-tide damage and to drain the extensive natural salt marshes to create farmland. Because the resulting agricultural lands surrounding the bay are fairly homogeneous, a list of species for any one of the numbered streets giving access to the bay could, with little modification, stand for all. Although the area is mostly agricultural, there has been considerable commercial intrusion in recent years. Several extremely large greenhouse complexes have been erected, a highly controversial golf course was developed on 72nd Street, and several very large private dwellings have appeared. All these have been sited on rough field terrain that comprised some of the best raptor foraging areas. In addition to these recent developments, there is also the Boundary Bay Airport and the smaller private Delta Air Park, at the south end of 104th Street. The OWL Wildlife Rehabilitation Centre (for raptors) is also on 72nd Street.

Directions

General access to the Boundary Bay area is from Highway 99, taking exit #20 to Highway 10 (also called Ladner Trunk Road) and Hornby Drive at the Mathews Exchange. Just after exiting, turn right at the traffic light onto Highway 10 to reach 88th Street and lower-numbered streets. To reach 96th Street and higher-numbered streets, go straight through the traffic light onto Hornby Drive, which curves eastwards after a short distance. Highway 10 and Hornby Drive run east-west, paralleling Highway 99 on its south side.

Note: Private vehicles are not permitted on the dykes; you must either walk, cycle or ride a horse. *Parking in this entire area is strictly limited,* and is provided *only* at the south ends of 64th, 72nd and 104th streets. The parking at 104th Street is in the parking lot of the Delta Air Park.

Bird Species

64TH STREET

Turn south off Highway 10 and drive through the housing development for .8 km (.5 mi). South of this is agricultural land. To the left are several sets of power lines and poles. **Red-tailed Hawks** and **Northern Harriers** use them for roosting and hunting perches. In winter and migration, you can find **Rough-legged Hawks** and **Peregrine Falcons**. All five falcon species use this area in winter or in migration, but **Prairie Falcons** are extremely rare. **Barn Owls** used to be relatively common throughout the area, but have been declining in recent years.

In spring and fall migrations, both **Pacific** and **American golden-plovers** in small numbers and **American Pipits** may use these fields. Wintering waterfowl use them as grazing lands, and shorebird flocks displaced by the bay's high tides await lower water, sometimes in very large standing roosts. At the 3.8-km (2.4-mi) mark, the railway right-of-way offers a slight rise from which to scan the surrounding fields, fence posts and hedgerows for **Northern Shrikes**. The ditches along the tracks often contain waterfowl at any time of the year, but in spring and summer are home to nesting **Blue-winged** and **Cinnamon teal**. A further .6 km (.4 mi) leads to a large commercial greenhouse on the left where winter flocks of **Red-**

winged and **Brewer's blackbirds** and **European Starlings** may occasionally harbour a **Yellow-headed Blackbird** or an even rarer **Rusty Blackbird** (see also 96th Street), with a handful of overwintering **Brown-headed Cowbirds**. At the south end of the road, check the hedgerows on both sides for mixed flocks of wintering and migrant **sparrows**. **Golden-crowned**, **White-crowned** and **Savannah sparrows** are relatively common, whereas **Lincoln's**, **Vesper**, **American Tree**, **White-throated** and **Harris's sparrows** are regular rarities in habitat such as this throughout the Vancouver Checklist Area.

On the foreshore on an average winter day, you can see flocks of tens of thousands of **Dunlin**, sometimes mixed with a small proportion of **Sanderling**; a thorough search may turn up one or two wintering **Western Sandpipers**. Huge numbers of **American Wigeon** and **Green-winged Teal**, with smaller numbers of **Northern Pintails** and **Mallards**, will also be here. **Eurasian Wigeon** are regular in these flocks and seem to be increasing in numbers. On overcast days, **Short-eared Owls** sometimes quarter the foreshore with the more common **Northern Harriers**, while **Red-tailed** and **Rough-legged hawks** circle overhead. **Bald Eagles** are surprisingly numerous, usually standing along the waterline. **Peregrine Falcons** regularly hunt along the foreshore, and there is the possibility of a **Gyrfalcon** appearing here. (A **Prairie Falcon** has been observed here in a few winters, but this may well have been a single individual.) In spring and fall there are large flocks of **Black-bellied Plovers** and **Western Sandpipers** along the foreshore, usually tide-displaced from feeding areas at the eastern end of the bay. **Northern Shrikes** are regular from October in small numbers. Examine any thickets along the dyke for wintering and migrant passerines.

Caution: The salt marsh is fragile. Please stay on the obvious trails.

36TH AVENUE

This east-west road connects 64th and 72nd Streets 1.5 km (.9 mi) south of Highway 10. Along its south side, the ploughed fields offer good habitat for **Black-bellied Plovers** and **golden-plovers**,

American Pipits, *Lapland Longspurs* and, more rarely, *Snow Buntings*. Gull flocks occasionally use these fields as standing roosts.

72ND STREET

Immediately south of Highway 10, hedgerows on both sides of the road offer good songbird habitat and are productive all year. In winter, the fields beyond these hedgerows sometimes contain large standing roosts of *gulls* sated from feeding in the Vancouver Landfill about 2 km (1.2 mi) to the north. (Gull enthusiasts take note: landfill management does not allow birding within the landfill.) These roosts mainly contain *Glaucous-winged*, *Mew* and *Thayer's gulls*, with *Herring* and *California gulls* in small numbers. *Western*, *Glaucous*, *Slaty-backed* and possibly *Iceland gulls* are uncommon to very rare. *Ring-billed Gulls* have become an abundant summer bird. These fields, extending south to the railway tracks, are also good raptor habitat. The dense rows of hawthorn trees adjacent to the road provide sheltered roosts and abundant food for fruit-eating species. Occasionally *Long-eared Owls* can be found there on winter days.

On the west side of 72nd Street and south of the railway is a large turf farm with extensive fields of short grass. This location is Vancouver's likeliest for *Buff-breasted Sandpipers*, which may pass through in August/September, but not every year. In addition, both species of *golden-plovers*, *Baird's Sandpipers* and potentially many other vagrant species may turn up. Please keep in mind that this is private land and must be scanned from the roadside.

In winter, check the irrigation machinery for perched raptors, including *Snowy Owls*. South of the railway on the left side is the Boundary Bay Airport, another excellent wintering raptor area, particularly for *Rough-legged Hawks* and *Short-eared Owls*. Just south of the airport, on the left, is the turnoff to the OWL Rehabilitation Centre, where there are a number of non-releasable raptors on public display.

Some 2.4 km (1.5 mi) south of Highway 10, on the left is the

1. West coast rain forest in Golden Ears Provincial Park

2. Viewing tower at Reifel Migratory Bird Sanctuary

3. Winter Gulls at 12th Avenue Lagoon in Boundary Bay Regional Park

4. Subalpine forest

5. Swans on Westham Island fields

6. Pelagic Cormorant
colony at Prospect Point
in Stanley Park

7. Great Blue Heron on a
rocky shoreline in
Stanley Park

8. Purple Martin nest
boxes on a "dolphin"
at Maplewood
Conservation Area

9. Snow Geese at Reifel Migratory Bird Sanctuary

10. Sandhill Crane at Reifel Migratory Bird Sanctuary

11. Dowitchers

Benson Home, a heritage farmhouse, at the intersection of 72nd Street and 36th Avenue. Its gardens, fruit trees and surrounding hedgerows offer cover for flocks of wintering **songbirds**. The barns and farmyards across from the Benson house attract very large flocks of **European Starlings** and wintering **icterids**. **Rusty** and **Yellow-headed blackbirds** have both occurred here in fall migration. In the next kilometre, in a field to the right, a large radio/microwave tower provides a good raptor perch. At the end of the road are hedgerows that may contain many wintering and migrant **sparrows**.

On the foreshore marsh and along the waterline, you can scan roosting shorebird and waterfowl flocks. About 1.5 km (.9 mi) east along the dyke is a thicket, which has harboured wintering **Yellow-rumped Warblers** with the more usual sparrows. Wintering **Western Meadowlarks** and sometimes **Sandhill Cranes** use the fields in this vicinity.

Snowy Owls can sometimes be found throughout the Fraser delta, but in years when they are scarce, the foreshore near the south end of 72nd Street is often the most likely place to find them.

BOUNDARY BAY AIRPORT ACCESS ROAD

Approaching from the north, turn left (east) off 72nd Street. The brushy strip between the road and the railway provides excellent cover and food for wintering songbirds, including **Northern Shrikes**. Potentially, you can see almost any raptor species in this general area and there may be flocks of gulls roosting in some of the fields. Scan from the roadside—most of the land here is posted No Trespassing. There are washrooms and a restaurant open to the public in the airport terminal.

96TH STREET

The high-tide line moves progressively closer to the dyke, squeezing the foreshore salt marsh into an increasingly narrow fringe towards 112th Street and making closer views of shorebirds and waterfowl possible. Half a kilometre (.3 mi) south from Hornby Drive on 96th is Cambridge Stables on the left, where large wintering **blackbird** and **starling flocks** gather, joined by the occasional **Yellow-headed Blackbird** and a few **Brown-headed Cowbirds**. **Rusty Blackbirds** have wintered here. On the right, a row of dense conifers offers owl roost possibilities, and **Bald Eagles** often perch at the top of large Douglas-fir trees, where they are visible for many kilometres.

On the dyke, about midway between 88th and 96th streets, there is a large and opulent private residence referred to by local birders as "the Mansion." A small lagoon here, the outflow channel of a pumping station, provides one of the very best shorebird sites in the Vancouver area. Some of the interesting birds seen here include **Green Herons**, **Stilt** and **Sharp-tailed sandpipers**, **Marbled Godwit** and **Red Knot**.

Remember that there is no parking at either 88th or 96th streets, necessitating a walk or cycle of about 5 km (3 mi) return from the Delta Air Park on 104th Street.

104TH STREET

From the corner of Hornby Drive, large conifers and gardens on either side provide good cover for **songbirds** and perches for **raptors**. A small woodlot and hedgerows at the end of the road often conceal the usual mixed flock of **sparrows** and, in migration, other passerines, such as **warblers**. The water line can be very close to the dyke at this point, making it a good location from which to scan **waterfowl flocks** and large groups of **shorebirds** displaced from their feeding areas to the east by rising tides.

112TH STREET

Remember that there is no parking at the south end of 112th Street. Walking or bicycling from 104th Street is warranted here, especially at migration times, since this is one of the best birding areas on Boundary Bay. Check the fields for **Cattle Egrets** in October and November. A short distance to the right (west), along the dyke, is a modern pump house and drainage outflow. The grating over the outflow is sometimes the fishing perch of a **Green Heron**. Many shorebirds use this area except at high tide: **Least**, **Western** and

Semipalmated sandpipers occur on the rocks, algal mats and floating debris bordering the channel; *Greater* and *Lesser yellowlegs*, and sometimes *Solitary Sandpipers*, on the muddy shores of the channel; *Black-bellied* and *Semipalmated plovers*, farther out towards the tide line. *Loons, grebes* and *diving ducks* frequently come up the channel almost to the dyke. On the dyke to the east, walk around a low metal gate and scan the narrow, sandy bars projecting seawards (east) from the foreshore for several hundred metres. Large concentrations of *gulls, shorebirds* and *waterfowl* gather here, joined in summer by *Caspian Terns*.

Water birds found here in summer include *Common Loons, Mallards, Gadwall* and *White-winged* and *Surf scoters*. Winter brings sometimes-large numbers of *Common* and *Red-throated loons* with small numbers of *Pacific Loons* (far more numerous off Point Roberts to the southwest). *Horned, Western* and *Red-necked grebes*, huge numbers of *American Wigeon, Northern Pintails, Green-winged Teal* and *Mallards* may be inshore, and great rafts of all three *scoter* species, *Long-tailed Ducks, Common* and *Red-breasted mergansers* and both *scaup* species can also be found here. *Pelagic* and *Double-crested cormorants* are common. *Brant* feed in small numbers on eelgrass beds here, though their main staging area is farther west, off Beach Grove and Roberts Bank.

The foreshore of Boundary Bay east of 112th offers some of the best shorebirding in western Canada, particularly in the fall migration from late June until late October. In spring and fall migrations, one can see flocks of tens of thousands of *Western Sandpipers* (a large proportion of the world's population) plus flocks of up to several thousand *Black-bellied Plovers*. In the multitude you may spot many other species, from *Long-billed Dowitchers* and *Semipalmated Plovers* to more unusual rarities such as *Stilt Sandpipers, Red Knots, Ruddy Turnstones* and *Hudsonian Godwits*. (*Bar-tailed Godwits* have been seen in several years.) A few accidentals such as *Snowy Plovers, Little* and *Red-necked stints* and Canada's first (and, so far, only) *Eastern Curlew* have also been sighted here.

One of the best places on Boundary Bay to view these large gatherings is the head of a large grassy spit almost 1 km (.6 mi) east of 112th Street. Take a trail that diverges diagonally right across the marsh towards the spit. From here you have an unobstructed view of Mud Bay, the main feeding ground. The enormous mass of Mount Baker looming in the distance on the usually clear days provides an awesome backdrop to the scene. Where there are shorebirds there are *falcons* to hunt them. Search the foreshore and the dead trees at the seaward edge of the woodlot just north of the grassy spit for perched falcons. Sometimes **Sharp-shinned** and **Cooper's hawks** or roosting **Great Horned** and **Barn owls** also use this woodlot, and it sometimes harbours good numbers of migrating passerines in spring. Transient **Ospreys** are regular here, especially in fall.

Eastwards from the woodlot, the dyke passes some dense bramble patches that provide excellent cover for wintering passerines. Farther on, the dyke runs very close to Highway 99, and **raptors** may be perched in the scattered trees. One particular large cottonwood seems almost always to have some eagle, hawk or falcon keeping watch on things. There are a few records from the east end of the bay of northbound **Golden Eagles**.

Written by Michael Price; revised by Carlo Giovanella

16. Serpentine Fen

Serpentine Fen is situated in South Surrey between the Serpentine River on the north and the Nicomekl River on the south. It is bordered by Highway 99 on the west and 99A on the east. The fen covers an area of 106 ha (262 a), which includes 80 ha (198 a) of dyked freshwater marsh and 4 ha (10 a) of undyked salt marsh. The remainder is mostly hay fields and brushy patches.

The present area is owned by the provincial government, having been cut off from surrounding farms by construction of the freeway. The fen is managed by the province and, over the years, has been used by Douglas College for farming, for various research schemes, and by the White Rock and Surrey Naturalists for educational tours. Ducks Unlimited (Canada) have their office on the property and have made considerable changes to drainage patterns and excavated large ponds for waterfowl. The dykes have been widened, and changes to the area are ongoing.

Vegetation consists mostly of small trees and bushes, which are plentiful, especially around the parking lot and down the lane, which was 44th Avenue. Many of these plantings were done by the White Rock and Surrey Naturalists Society. Blackberries, elderberries, Pacific crabapples and mountain ash berries all provide good food for birds. Some ponds have large patches of cattails. Fruit trees can be found near the Ducks Unlimited building.

There is a public trail network along most principal dykes and three viewing towers with good views of marsh and river habitats and fields. The trails are flat, providing very easy walking. Mammals to be seen include muskrats, coyotes and rabbits. Harbour seals can be found in the tidal Serpentine River.

Directions

From Vancouver, take Highway 99 (Oak Street) south through the George Massey Tunnel and on as the highway curves to the east, turning off at the sign for White Rock (exit #10). Almost immediately, turn left onto Highway 99A north (King George Highway). Keep in the left lane and follow King George Highway for approximately 2.4 km (1.5 mi). Turn left at 44th Avenue (a small country lane) beside Art Knapp's Plantland. Follow this dirt lane to the parking lot on the left. There are picnic tables here, but no toilet facilities anywhere at the fen.

Bird Species

Much of the birding at the fen depends on water levels as, in a dry summer, local farmers use the Serpentine River for irrigation.

Scopes are recommended, as you can't get close to most ponds. Over 175 species have been recorded in the immediate area of the fen. Of these, about 50 are listed as rare, casual or accidental.

Start your bird walk by going left (west) from the parking lot down the lane. There are swallow boxes along the way and *Tree*, *Violet-green* and *Barn swallows* are plentiful over the ponds and on the wires. The bushes and trees along the lane are good for *Northern Flickers* and *Downy Woodpeckers*. *Steller's Jays*, *Black-capped Chickadees*, *Bushtits*, *Bewick's Wrens*, *American Robins*, *Song*, *White-crowned* and *Golden-crowned sparrows*, *Spotted Towhees*, *Ruby-crowned Kinglets*, *House* and *Purple finches* and *Red-winged* and *Brewer's blackbirds* can all be seen almost all year round. *Willow Flycatchers*, *Cedar Waxwings*, *Orange-crowned*, *Yellow*, *Yellow-rumped* and *Wilson's warblers* and *Brown-headed Cowbirds* are more common in spring and summer, as are *Rufous Hummingbirds*. In fall and winter look for *Northern Shrikes* and *Evening Grosbeaks*. At the end of the lane, the trail turns north. Look up here to see what the power line towers have to offer. *Red-tailed Hawks* are present year round. *American Kestrels* may be here in spring and fall, and *Sharp-shinned*, *Cooper's* and *Rough-legged hawks* can be found in winter. *Northern Harriers* are common all year over the fields and *Bald Eagles* are seen frequently.

The ponds to the west of the trail sometimes have *Blue-winged* and *Cinnamon teal* in the spring and summer. Climb the viewing tower here for a good overview of ponds to the west and east. *Great Blue Herons* and *Ring-necked Pheasants* are common all year. *Canada Geese*, *Green-winged Teal*, *Mallards*, *Northern Pintails*, *Northern Shovelers*, *American Wigeon* and *American Coots* are present most of the year. *Glaucous-winged Gulls* can always be seen, while *Ring-billed*, *Bonaparte's* and *Mew gulls* are common seasonally. *Short-eared Owls* are a possibility, but they are uncommon now, as are the *Barn Owls* that once lived in the collapsed barn.

From the viewing tower, turn east along the Serpentine River dyke, keeping an eye out for birds on the river, especially when

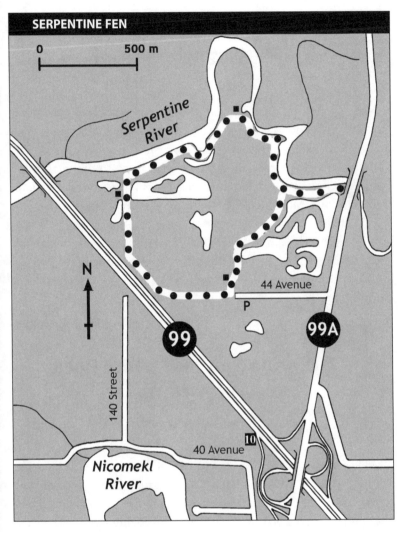

SERPENTINE FEN

0   500 m

Serpentine River

N

99

99A

44 Avenue

P

140 Street

40 Avenue   10

Nicomekl River

the tide is in. *Common Loons* and *Western* and *Horned grebes* are seen in the fall and winter, and *Double-crested Cormorants* are present year round. *Common Mergansers*, *Buffleheads*, *Common Goldeneyes* and *Ruddy Ducks* appear at times. *Belted Kingfishers* patrol the river. When there is enough mud around the ponds, search the shorelines for shorebirds, keeping an eye out for something unusual, as this is where most of the rarities in the fen occur.

In total, 32 shorebird species have been observed at the fen. **Greater Yellowlegs** and **Killdeer** are frequent except in winter. **American Avocets**, **Black-necked Stilts** and **Ruffs** have visited occasionally in the past.

Climb the next tower for a look around and in spring try the bushes along the inside of the dyke for **warblers** and other migrants. After following the dyke almost to the highway, you will notice a small footbridge over the ditch to the south. Follow this trail, which gives a good view of the large pond to the east. In the cattails look and listen for the many **Marsh Wrens** and **Common Yellowthroats**. **Savannah Sparrows** like this area, too.

There is just one more tower to climb before reaching the parking lot and completing the circuit. If you are still wanting more, check the bushes down the lane to the east. Sometimes the old orchard near the Ducks Unlimited building is good for **warblers** and **woodpeckers**.

Written and revised by Jack Williams

17. Blackie Spit and White Rock Waterfront

Blackie Spit (at the extreme north end of Crescent Beach) and the City of White Rock are situated about 30 km (19 mi) from downtown Vancouver on the Semiahmoo (sem-ee-AH-moo) Peninsula, in the southwest part of Surrey. The peninsula is bounded to the west by Mud Bay and Boundary Bay, and to the south by Semiahmoo Bay. Most of the land on the peninsula has been developed for residential use.

Some 5,000 years ago, the peninsula was inhabited by Coast Salish peoples. When Captain George Vancouver anchored his ship *Discovery* in the bay in 1792, a populous village of the Semiahmoo band flourished at the mouth of the small river, which empties into the bay just north of the present-day international boundary. Members of the band still live on the Semiahmoo Indian Reserve at the mouth of the (Little) Campbell River. A large boulder, a relic of the Ice Age on White Rock's East Beach, was used as a navigational aid. The rock, limed white with guano, eventually gave the city its name. The rock's white appearance is now maintained with paint.

European settlement began in the mid-1800s. By 1910, White Rock was being promoted as a resort area because of its mild climate and sandy beaches. A cottage community sprang up along the Semiahmoo Bay waterfront. Today, White Rock city encompasses almost 8 square km (3 square mi) and is surrounded by the southern portion of Surrey.

Blackie Spit

Blackie Spit (once the site of an Indian encampment) was settled by Walter Blackie in 1871. He farmed the land on which the community of Crescent Beach is now situated. Today, Blackie Spit refers to the sandy point jutting into Mud Bay (the shallow northeastern part of Boundary Bay), at the mouth of the Nicomekl River, and adjacent undeveloped land.

The vegetation consists of various salt- and sand-tolerant grasses, shrubs such as red elderberry, common snowberry, Indian-plum, and Nootka rose, along with introduced Himalayan blackberry and Scotch broom. Trees include Pacific crabapple, Pacific willow, paper birch, black cottonwood, Saskatoon, black hawthorn and introduced English hawthorn. Glasswort thrives in the saltwater marsh areas.

Directions

To reach Blackie Spit by car from Vancouver, take Highway 99 south. After passing through Richmond and the George Massey Tunnel, the highway curves eastward and passes close to the north shore of Mud Bay. Take the White Rock/Crescent Beach exit (#10) and bear right, following the signs to Crescent Beach. You will now be on Crescent Road. After about 5 km (3.1 mi), Crescent Road descends a hill and crosses a railway track. At a V-intersection just beyond the tracks, bear right onto Sullivan Street. Turn right again onto McBride Avenue (the last street before the beach) and follow it to the end to reach the Blackie Spit parking area. The gate is open from about 8 A.M. to dusk. If you arrive before 8 A.M., park outside and walk in.

Blackie Spit can also be reached from downtown Vancouver by the #351 Crescent Beach bus, which provides service to Sullivan Street and McBride Avenue. Buses run every 1/2 hour on weekdays, and hourly during evenings, weekends and holidays.

The White Rock and Surrey Naturalists Society operates an information centre in Beecher Place, at the foot of Beecher Street in Crescent Beach, on weekends, October through May, from 1 to 5 P.M. Washrooms, open all year from 8 A.M. to dusk, are also located in Beecher Place.

Bird Species

Almost 200 species have been recorded in the Blackie Spit/Crescent Beach area. Birding is best during migration periods and in winter, although rarities can show up in any season. Midsummer is the quietest period, when *Barn*, *Violet-green* and *Tree swallows*, *White-crowned Sparrows*, *House Finches*, *Northwestern Crows*, *European Starlings*, *Red-winged Blackbirds* and *House Sparrows* are the most numerous species.

It is wise to check tide levels (see "Tides," page 71) before your trip to Blackie Spit. Tide levels are very important when looking for *water birds* and *shorebirds*, which predominate in this area. Make sure you arrive at least an hour (two hours is even better) before high tide for optimum viewing. At low tide, any water birds present will likely be too far out to be seen adequately, if at all.

Explore the centre of Blackie Spit, as well as both shorelines. *Savannah Sparrows* are common breeders here and may be found

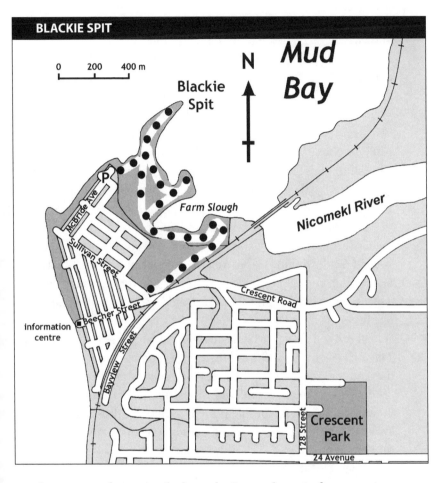

BLACKIE SPIT

0   200   400 m

N

Mud Bay

Blackie Spit

Farm Slough

Nicomekl River

McBride Ave

Sullivan Street

Beecher Street

Bayview Street

information centre

Crescent Road

128 Street

Crescent Park

24 Avenue

in the grasses from April through September. A few transient *Lapland Longspurs* (September and October) and **Snow Buntings** (November and December) are sometimes seen. Watch for large flocks of shorebirds such as **Dunlin, Sanderling** and **Black-bellied Plovers** from fall through late spring. Offshore, **Common Loons** may be seen at any season, although they are most abundant from fall through spring. In winter, **Red-throated Loons** are uncommon, and **Yellow-billed Loons** are rare. **Horned, Red-necked** and **Western grebes** are likely to be found from fall through spring. Off the west side of the spit, diving ducks are usually abundant from fall through spring; look for **Buffleheads**, **Common Goldeneyes**, **Surf Scoters** and **Greater Scaup** (sometimes in very large rafts), along with smaller numbers of **Long-tailed Ducks**, **Barrow's Goldeneyes** and **Common** and **Red-breasted mergansers**. You may spot a few **Canvasbacks**, **Lesser Scaup** and **White-winged** and **Black scoters**.

The saltwater marsh across the Nicomekl River mouth, opposite Blackie Spit, is used by loafing **gulls**, **Great Blue Herons**, resident **Canada Geese** and sometimes **Bald Eagles**. At times it may teem with shorebirds. Harbour seals haul out regularly on certain islets. There is no public access to that area; view it by telescope from Blackie Spit. *Do not attempt to cross on the railway trestle.*

The shallow, sheltered waters off the east side of the spit are attractive to wintering dabbling ducks. **Northern Pintails**, **Green-winged Teal**, **Mallards** and **American Wigeon** are abundant from fall through spring. Search among the wigeon for **Eurasian Wigeon**; usually one or more can be found. **Double-crested Cormorants** rest on the pilings. **Gulls** like to loaf in the marshy area along the east side of the spit; look for **Glaucous-winged** (at any season), **Mew** and **Thayer's** (winter) and **Ring-billed gulls** (summer). From late summer into fall, be alert for the possibility of a **Franklin's Gull** among the flocks of **Bonaparte's Gulls**. Transient **California Gulls** appear in small numbers in spring and fall. Watch and listen for **Caspian Terns** (May to September) and **Common Terns** (May and August through September).

If peaceful flocks of feeding or resting ducks, shorebirds, gulls or terns suddenly erupt into flight, the reason for the disturbance may be the approach of a raptor. Look for a **Bald Eagle**, **Northern Harrier**, **Sharp-shinned**, **Cooper's** or **Red-tailed hawk**, **Peregrine Falcon** or **Merlin**.

A short distance south and east of the spit is a small tidal pond, surrounded by shrubs and trees, that attracts **White-crowned** and **Song sparrows**, **Black-capped Chickadees** and **Spotted Towhees** (at any season), along with **Dark-eyed Juncos**, **Golden-crowned Sparrows** and **Purple Finches** in winter. Transient **warblers** may include **Orange-crowned**, **Yellow-rumped** and **Wilson's**. At low tide it is possible to continue walking along the shore, across the narrow channel that fills and drains the pond, but at high tide you will have to detour around the west side of the pond. In either case, after crossing an open sandy area, you will reach Farm Slough, a shallow backwater of the Nicomekl River. At the optimal tidal levels of 3.4 to 4 m (11 to 13 ft), this sheltered slough may be full of *shorebirds* or *ducks*. A good viewing spot is at the north side of the slough's mouth, marked by a row of low pilings, remnants of an old oyster cannery. From this point, you may scan both Farm Slough and the Nicomekl estuary. Another good viewing point is from the south end of the row of pilings on the opposite side of the slough. *Common Yellowthroats* and *Yellow Warblers* nest in shrubby vegetation around the slough; one or two *Belted Kingfishers* might come along in any season.

The main northward migration of shorebirds is compressed into approximately mid-April to mid-May; numbers may be fairly small, and their presence brief. The main southward migration in fall (July through September) produces the greatest variety of shorebirds, but some species are present all year. *Killdeer* are resident in the area and may be found at any season. Small flocks of *Greater Yellowlegs* and *Long-billed Dowitchers* can usually be found. Some non-breeding *Whimbrels* may linger in the vicinity all summer. A few *Semipalmated Plovers* and *Semipalmated Sandpipers* may be found in late summer among the abundant *Western* and common *Least sandpipers*. Such locally rare shorebirds as *Willets*, *Hudsonian* and *Marbled godwits* and *Long-billed Curlews* have all been seen here on a number of occasions.

On the south side of Farm Slough, a narrow, rough path leads along the wooded dyke bordering the slough. This is a good area for resident passerines, such as *sparrows*, *finches*, *robins*, *Pine Siskins*, *American Goldfinches* and *Bushtits*, as well as transient species. The rough path joins the gravel walking path atop a wider, parallel dyke on the southern side of the slough's mouth. Pass the pump house, bear right (south), and walk along an unnamed road that parallels the railway tracks on the south side of Dunsmuir Farm

Community Gardens. Scan the garden fields for a **Northern Shrike** (casual) in winter. The road is lined by dense shrub thickets and a few Lombardy poplars, in which one or two pairs of **Bullock's Orioles** usually nest in summer.

White Rock Waterfront

The City of White Rock has developed a promenade 2.2 km (1.4 mi) long, along the East and West beaches. The two beaches are divided by the wooden pier, which extends almost 500 m (1,650 ft) southwards into Semiahmoo Bay. The promenade and the pier are heavily used year round.

Directions

To reach the White Rock waterfront from Vancouver via Highway 99 south, take the 8th Avenue exit (#3) onto Highway 99A (King George Highway), then turn right (west) onto 8th Avenue. After several blocks, 8th Avenue becomes Marine Drive. Pay parking lots are located at frequent intervals along the drive.

Bird Species

In summer, resident **Canada Geese**, **Mallards**, **Double-crested Cormorants**, **Great Blue Herons** and one or two **Belted Kingfishers** may be seen. A few non-breeding **Common Loons** may be present, far out in the bay. **Northwestern Crows**, **Glaucous-winged** and **Ring-billed gulls** and perhaps a few non-breeding **Bonaparte's Gulls** loaf on the beaches. Watch and listen for **Caspian Terns**. Resident raptors include **Bald Eagles** and **Red-tailed Hawks**.

Transient species include **Red-necked Grebes** (sometimes in very large numbers), **Western** and **Least sandpipers** (April and May; July through September), and **Brant** (March and April). A subspecies of Brant, the **Gray-bellied Brant**, has been occurring in the Pacific Northwest in increasing numbers and is worth noting.

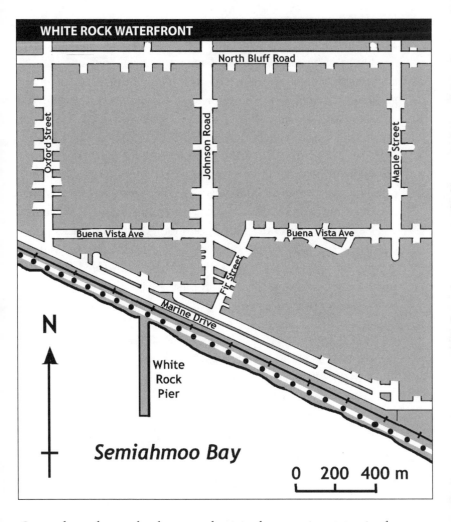

Currently under study, they may be raised to species status in the future. **Parasitic Jaegers** (casual in May and August to September) sometimes are seen harassing **Bonaparte's Gulls** and **Common Terns** over the bay.

Winter is the best time to look for birds in the waters of the bay, when large numbers of wintering waterfowl are present. Depending on the tide (mid-level to high tide is best), weather, wind and other variables known only to birds, **loons**, **grebes** and **ducks** may be plentiful. Scrutinize the rock breakwater at the end of the pier for **Black Turnstones**. Watch for **Bald Eagles** overhead. **Common Loons** are found easily, **Red-throated Loons** are considered uncommon, and **Pacific Loons** are uncommon to rare. **Western** and **Horned grebes** are common, while **Red-necked Grebes** are fairly common. Look carefully for an **Eared Grebe**; one or more winter in the bay every year. **Canada Geese** are seen often. Common duck species include **Mallards**, **Northern Pintails**, **American Wigeon** (a **Eurasian Wigeon** could be with them), **Greater** and **Lesser scaup**, **Common** and **Barrow's goldeneyes**, **Buffleheads**, **Surf** and **White-winged scoters** and **Ruddy Ducks**. **Harlequin Ducks**, **Long-tailed Ducks** and **mergansers** are fairly common. The diving ducks prefer the deeper water and rocky offshore terrain west of the pier and the West Beach. **Alcids**, such as **Common Murres**, **Marbled Murrelets** and **Pigeon Guillemots**, are rare and usually far offshore. An assortment of wintering **gulls**, mostly **Glaucous-winged**, **Mew** and **Ring-billed**, loiter about the pier and beaches. Check carefully for **Thayer's Gulls** and perhaps a **Western** or a **Herring gull**. Shorebirds are few, but watch for **Dunlin**, **Sanderling** and **Greater Yellowlegs**. **Black-bellied Plovers** are sometimes seen, usually just flying by.

Safety Note: Although local residents reach the shores east and west of the promenade by walking on the Burlington Northern Railway tracks, the practice is *dangerous and not recommended*. There are several blind corners, and the trains, though infrequent, are fast and quiet. Furthermore, track walkers risk being charged with trespass by railway police.

Written and revised by Hue and Jo Ann MacKenzie

12. Black Oystercatcher

13. Harlequin Ducks on a rocky shoreline

16. Hooded Merganser
at Lost Lagoon

17. Chestnut-backed Chickadee

18. Spotted Towhee

19. Band-tailed Pigeon

20. Snowy Owl at
Boundary Bay
(Below left)

21. Red-breasted
Sapsucker

18. Iona and Sea Islands

One of the west coast's premier birding locations, Iona Island is situated near Vancouver International Airport, less than 30 minutes' drive from downtown. The area owes its incredible diversity to the sewage treatment plant, whose ponds allow birders to observe **sandpipers** and **waterfowl** up close, and whose discharge pipe, the South Jetty, provides observation points over the Strait of Georgia.

The island was first settled in 1885 by the McMillan family, who named it after their Scottish home. The North Jetty, which attracts many species of shorebirds, was built between 1917 and 1935, and has unique dune vegetation introduced from Oregon. Prior to 1958, when the causeway connecting Sea and Iona islands was completed, the only access to Iona Island was by boat. The sewage treatment plant and the South Jetty were completed in 1961, and an upgrade to the sewage plant's discharge pipe, completed in 1988, formed the present 4-km-long (2.5-mi) South Jetty. The Greater Vancouver Regional District now oversees the public areas of the island, known as Iona Beach Regional Park. In the early 1990s an area between the sewage ponds and the jetties became the new home for displaced **Yellow-headed Blackbirds** in a marsh habitat restoration project. This was a joint effort by the Vancouver Natural History Society, GVRD Parks and Environment Canada. The marsh had been damaged during construction to extend the sewage outflow pipe. The marsh and the "outer" pond, the beach area with its picnic tables, toilets and change-rooms, a large parking lot and a viewing tower at the base of the South Jetty are all part of the regional park.

In addition to the park, birders have access to the ponds at the sewage treatment plant. These are known as the "inner ponds," and you can get to them through the "birders' gate" (see below). A second gate in the west side of the fence now makes it possible to enter the marsh directly from the inner ponds and make a circular walk back to the gate via the road.

As with most urban parks, summer weekends bring out the crowds. If the jetties are busy, visit the sewage ponds, which are open to birders only. You can still scan the public ponds from the private side of the fence.

Directions

At the time of writing, the maze of intersections and overpasses at the south end of the Arthur Laing Bridge is under construction and changes in the traffic patterns occur every few months. Consult a good current city map before setting out, and in general, follow signs first towards Vancouver International Airport, and then watch for the green and yellow GVRD Parks signs directing you to Iona Beach Regional Park. The park is approximately 7.5 km (4.7 mi) from these intersections. As airport expansion activities will keep this area in a state of flux for several years, even frequent visitors will find changes in the route from time to time.

To get to the Arthur Laing Bridge from downtown Vancouver, take Granville Street south (past 70th Street where it curves left) onto the bridge. If coming to Iona from the south on Highway 99, or from the east on Highway 91, follow the signs for Vancouver International Airport and watch for the signs for Iona Beach Regional Park. Whichever route you take, you will eventually drive under the Arthur Laing Bridge and head west past the airport on Grauer and Ferguson roads towards Iona Island. These roads are on Sea Island, a large part of which is covered by Vancouver International Airport. Partway along Ferguson Road the only right (north) turn is at McDonald Road. This leads a short distance to McDonald Beach, where there are boat launch facilities and washrooms. At the end of Ferguson Road, across the causeway that links Sea Island and Iona Island, you will find Iona Beach Regional Park.

This area is not served by public transportation, but cycling the roads on Sea and Iona islands is very easy—it's all flat land! However, you will have to brave heavy city traffic to get there.

Bird Species

Iona Island and vicinity has an ever-growing checklist of over 300 confirmed species, including 49 species of shorebirds, thanks to the variety of habitats available and the tolerance of the sewage treatment plant authorities towards eager birders searching for the rare and unusual. Happily, Iona Island is noted for these.

SEA ISLAND

After driving under the Arthur Laing Bridge, follow Grauer and Ferguson roads towards Iona Island. Visitors to the west coast in winter should check any gulls or wigeon in the fields adjacent to Grauer Road for **Eurasian Wigeon**, **Mew Gulls** and **Thayer's Gulls**, all of which frequent this area. A walk along the north dyke (which runs along the North Arm of the Fraser River) often produces **Black-capped Chickadees**, **Bushtits** and **Spotted Towhees** at any time of year and **Song**, **Fox** and other **sparrows** in winter. You can walk west on the north dyke (no car access) from a small gravel parking area to the right off Grauer Road, or either east or west from McDonald Beach, where there is a large parking area. A walk along McDonald Road is also good for these species, for **Green Herons** in late summer and for **Willow Flycatchers** and

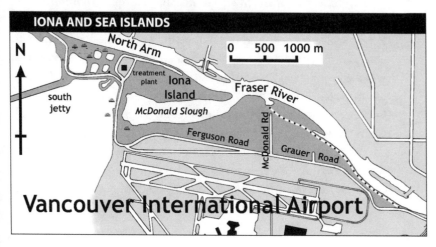

Black-headed Grosbeaks in spring and summer. Shrubby areas near the entrance to McDonald Beach Park and at the small woodlot by the intersection of Ferguson Road and the causeway are often frequented by *Bewick's Wrens*. *Rufous Hummingbirds* can often be seen along McDonald Road and along the portion of the north dyke near the small woodlot mentioned above.

The fields on either side of Grauer and Ferguson roads are hunted all year by *Northern Harriers* and *Red-tailed Hawks* and, in winter, by *Rough-legged Hawks* and sometimes *Short-eared Owls*. The airport fence and small trees and shrubs along the road are worth checking in winter for *American Kestrels*, *Northern Shrikes* and *Western Meadowlarks*, while *Savannah Sparrows* are common in the fields in summer. Marshy areas throughout Sea Island host numerous *Marsh Wrens* all year and *Common Yellowthroats* in spring and summer. *Great Blue Herons* can be seen virtually anywhere any time, but in winter they are especially common in fields, where they hunt voles instead of their usual fishy fare!

CAUSEWAY

From Ferguson Road, turn right onto the causeway linking Sea and Iona islands. This is a good place to stop and look at *water birds*. The best time to be here is about one hour before high tide. Expect good numbers of *waterfowl*, *Great Blue Herons*, *shorebirds* and *gulls*. Across the road to the east is McDonald Slough. This is an excellent place year round to see roosting *gulls*. The log booms and pilings in the slough often host loafing *Double-crested Cormorants*, *Great Blue Herons*, *waterfowl* and sometimes flocks of *Dunlin*. *Red-throated Loons* and *Western Grebes* also sometimes frequent the slough in winter. *Virginia Rails* regularly call from both the salt marsh along the western edge of the causeway and the southwestern corner of the slough, especially around sunrise and sunset. During low tides, large flocks of shorebirds (especially *Dunlin* in winter and *Western Sandpipers* during migration periods) feed on the tidal flats, and *Caspian Terns* sometimes loaf there.

INNER PONDS

Continue along the causeway and follow the road to the left into the park. *Do not drive into the Sewage Treatment Plant parking lot.* Just past the yellow-gated entrance to the park, there is a parking area at the side of the road for birders. You will see the "birders' gate" in the fence on your right and a kiosk just inside the gate, which holds the sightings book and an Iona Island checklist. Feel free to sign the book with your day's observations or to check what has been seen in the area recently. If you intend to bird late in the day, take careful note of the park closing time posted near the yellow gate. If you think you might be late, park outside the gate, which is shut at closing time.

The officials at the sewage treatment plant have been very helpful to and tolerant of birders for over 25 years. Please respect their property and remember that there are no public facilities there. You are welcome to bird the inner sewage ponds at any time during daylight hours. From the kiosk, you will see a path through the grass to your left, leading to the four ponds. The levels of the inner ponds are controlled according to the demands of the plant. During the height of the shorebird migration, at least one pond is kept at an ideal level. Another pond will likely have one year's growth of vegetation and will host breeding **Soras**, **Virginia Rails** and possibly a pair of **Wilson's Phalaropes**. The sewage ponds are best known for their ability to attract **shorebirds**. They often number in the thousands and present an excellent possibility of finding rarities. On a rising tide, as the birds are pushed off the diminishing mud flats, they crowd into the ponds. Spring migration begins in early April, with numbers reaching a peak by mid-May. By the end of June a few northbound stragglers meet the vanguard of southbound returning adults.

The common spring shorebirds are **Western** and **Least sandpipers**, **Long-billed** and **Short-billed dowitchers**, **Semipalmated Plovers**, **Killdeer**, **Dunlin**, **Greater** and **Lesser yellowlegs** and **Common Snipe**. In the late spring, **Spotted Sandpipers** are present. Less common but seen every spring are **Semipalmated**, **Pectoral** and *Baird's sandpipers*, *American Golden-Plovers* and *Wilson's Phalaropes*.

Spring migration is fast and purposeful, unlike fall with its more leisurely pace. The first southbound *Western Sandpipers* appear in the last days of June. This is the best time to look for adult *Red-necked Stints*, which are rare but have occurred many times. Numbers of returning *Western Sandpipers* build up dramatically through July. Other common species at this time are *Least*, *Baird's*, *Pectoral* and *Semipalmated sandpipers*. As July gives way to August, the juvenile shorebirds start moving south. This time is always exciting as numbers and species start to diversify dramatically. By mid-September the ponds will be packed with a great variety of species. *Pectoral* and *Baird's sandpipers*, *Greater* and *Lesser yellowlegs* and *Wilson's* and *Red-necked phalaropes* are now more common. Less common but annual species are *Ruff*, *Solitary Sandpipers*, *Stilt Sandpipers*, *Marbled* and *Hudsonian godwits* and *Buff-breasted Sandpipers*. The vast numbers of shorebirds also attract other visitors to the ponds. Fall is an excellent time to see *Peregrine Falcons*, *Merlins*, *Cooper's Hawks* and *American Kestrels*. There is nothing more dramatic than watching a *Peregrine Falcon* chasing a huge flock of shorebirds—the sight is truly breathtaking.

By the beginning of October, the numbers of small shorebirds have diminished, but this is the time in which a rare, but regular, visitor from Siberia might appear at Iona. The best place outside Alaska to see juvenile *Sharp-tailed Sandpipers* every fall is at Iona. Along with the increase in *Pectoral Sandpipers* is an increase in the number of Sharp-tailed Sandpipers as well. Numbers of Sharp-tailed Sandpipers vary from year to year, but at least one turns up annually. As October ends, wintering flocks of *Dunlin* return in the thousands with small numbers of wintering *Western Sandpipers* mixed among them. Other shorebirds, which will stay for the winter in smaller numbers, include *Greater Yellowlegs*, *Long-billed Dowitchers*, *Common Snipe*, *Sanderling*, *Black-bellied Plovers* and *Killdeer*.

Iona's most famous visitor, the **Spoonbill Sandpiper**, was seen by hundreds of lucky people in late July 1978. Other rarities that have contributed to Iona's top status as a location to find rare shorebirds include **Black-necked Stilt**, **Snowy Plover**, **Upland Sandpiper**, **White-rumped Sandpiper**, **Little Stint**, **Great Knot**, **Curlew Sandpiper** and **Red Phalarope**. With 49 confirmed species of shorebirds, Iona Island is hard to beat anywhere on the west coast of North America.

Large numbers of waterfowl also frequent the sewage lagoon ponds, especially **Gadwall**, **Mallards**, **Northern Pintails**, **Northern Shovelers** and **Green-winged Teal** in winter, spring and fall, and **Blue-winged** and **Cinnamon teal** in spring. The northeastern pond is one of the most reliable places in the Vancouver area for visitors to find **Mew** and **Thayer's gulls** in winter.

Although the sewage ponds have an enviable reputation among birding hot spots, that reputation goes beyond shorebirds. All six species of **swallows** can be found here, large flocks of **American Pipits** pass through, and **Vaux's** and **Black swifts** are seen in approaching storm clouds. The row of trees and shrubs between the inner ponds and the outer pond and marsh sometimes harbours numerous passerines, notably **Spotted Towhees** and **Song**, **Fox**, **Lincoln's**, **White-crowned** and **Golden-crowned sparrows**, especially during migration and in winter. A few **warblers** may also be found here during migration. Some of the exciting non-shorebird finds over the years include **Garganey**, **Forster's Tern**, **Say's Phoebe**, **Northern Mockingbird**, **Sage Thrasher** and **Clay-colored** and **Harris's sparrows**.

OUTER POND AND MARSH

After birding the inner ponds, you may wish to walk through the gate in the western fence into the marsh and from there to the large outer pond (or you can return to your car and drive around to the main parking lot). The new marsh was designed to attract **Yellow-headed Blackbirds**, an uncommon species in the Vancouver area, which were displaced from another marsh during the course of airport expansion. The blackbird population has relocated success-fully to the present marsh and may be seen there from April until mid-August. Also present in the marsh are **Pied-billed Grebes**, **Virginia Rails**, **Marsh Wrens** and **Red-winged Blackbirds**.

The pond, with its several islands, is an excellent place to study ducks. Sometimes in the winter a **Tufted Duck** may be found in the large flocks of **Greater** and **Lesser scaup**. Look also for the occa-sional **Redhead** and **Ring-necked Duck**. **Ruddy Ducks** are almost always present in winter as well as **American Coots**, **Buffleheads** and one or two **Pied-billed Grebes**. In spring, **Cinnamon** and **Blue-winged teal** might be found here. The best time to see the outer pond full of waterfowl is from November to April during a high tide. During winter, **Mew Gulls** often bathe communally in this pond.

SOUTH JETTY

Vancouver's sewage, after treatment, is deposited more than 4 km (2.5 mi) offshore into the Strait of Georgia. Happily for birders, the means of transport is a sea-level jetty with an observation area at the far end. A gravel road makes bicycling an attractive alternative to the 8- km (5-mi) round trip on foot. Motorized vehicles are prohibited on the jetty. There is a portable washroom at the end and there are two wind shelters partway along the jetty. The weather can change very quickly, and visitors are advised to carry warm clothing, water and a snack.

Probably the most important consideration when visiting the South Jetty is the tide level, followed by the season. At low tide in the summer there may be little to interest birders. However, a rising tide in the fall can be very productive. From July to the end of October large numbers of **Western**, **Least** and **Semipalmated sand-pipers**, with smaller numbers of **Baird's** and **Pectoral sandpipers**, **Black** and **Ruddy turnstones** and **Surfbirds** may be seen. **Wandering Tattlers** sometimes also turn up at this time. Fall also brings return-ing **waterfowl** and **seabirds**. Migrating **Bonaparte's Gulls** and **Common Terns** will draw **Parasitic Jaegers**. These are most easily seen from the end of the jetty from late August through mid-

October as they harass the terns and gulls. Other specialty species that the South Jetty may produce are **Lapland Longspurs** and **Snow Buntings**. These usually appear in October.

Winter is the most productive time at the South Jetty. The multitude of species commonly observed includes **Common**, **Pacific** and **Red-throated loons**, **Western**, **Red-necked** and **Horned grebes**, **Double-crested** and **Pelagic cormorants**, **Great Blue Herons**, **Canada** and **Snow geese**, **Green-winged Teal**, **Greater** and **Lesser scaup**, **Surf**, **White-winged** and **Black scoters**, **Long-tailed Ducks**, **Barrow's** and **Common goldeneyes**, **Red-breasted Mergansers**, **Thayer's** and **Mew gulls** and **Dunlin**. Rarer but regularly seen species are **Eared Grebes**, **Greater White-fronted Geese**, **Brant**, **Eurasian Wigeon**, **Redheads**, **Ring-necked Ducks**, **Black Oystercatchers**, **Rock Sandpipers**, **Western Gulls**, **Pigeon Guillemots**, **Common Murres**, **Marbled** and **Ancient murrelets** and **Rhinoceros Auklets**.

Although birding from the jetty is good all winter, the chance of seeing local rarities increases dramatically during or just after a southerly or southeasterly storm system from May to early June or from July to November. Records exist for **Sooty Shearwaters**, **Common** and **King eiders**, **Little**, **Black-headed** and **Sabine's gulls** and **Black-legged Kittiwakes**.

NORTH JETTY

This sand-dune jetty, several kilometres long, is a worthwhile walk at any time, but is more rewarding from July to November. In season, the dune grasses provide habitat for nesting **Savannah Sparrows**, **Killdeer** and **Spotted Sandpipers**, and the first nest of a **Caspian Tern** in the Vancouver area was found here in 1995. From September to November, flocks of **Lapland Longspurs**, sometimes accompanied by **Horned Larks** or **Snow Buntings**, occur here. The best birding is on a rising tide when the birds are pushed towards the shoreline of the jetty. Larger shorebirds, such as **Black-bellied Plovers**, are more likely to be observed here than on the inner ponds. Rarer species such as **Marbled Godwits**, **Whimbrel**, **Red**

Knots and *American* and *Pacific golden-plovers* have all been seen in this area. At the very end of the sand dunes, another rock jetty extends for several more kilometres. *Walk this area only on a low tide and pay close attention to the turning tide to avoid being cut off.* A careful observer might be rewarded by views of shorebirds preferring rocky areas.

The mud flats between the two jetties are a good place to find loafing *Bonaparte's*, *Glaucous-winged* and *California gulls* and *Common* and *Caspian terns*. Sometimes a *Franklin's Gull* can be found in the fall among the mixed flocks.

From offshore alcids to the finer points of shorebird plumages, from winter "dickey-birding" to unravelling the mysteries of gulls—no matter what your birding interests, Iona Island holds the promise of good, and the possibility of exceptional, birding.

FRASER RIVER, MIDDLE ARM

If time permits, birders visiting in winter may wish to check the Middle Arm of the Fraser River before leaving Sea Island. The best spot is the vicinity of a breakwater west of the seaplane base at the intersection of Agar and Inglis drives. To get there, take Russ Baker Way south towards the No. 2 Road Bridge. Turn right from Russ Baker Way onto Inglis Drive, and follow it to its intersection with

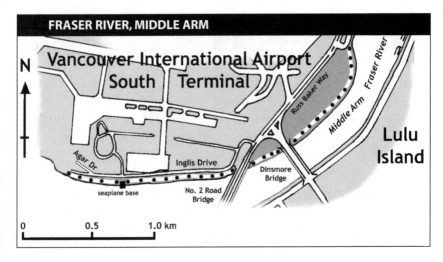

FRASER RIVER, MIDDLE ARM

Vancouver International Airport
South Terminal

Russ Baker Way

Middle Arm

Fraser River

Lulu
Island

Agar Dr

Inglis Drive

Dinsmore
Bridge

seaplane base

No. 2 Road
Bridge

0   0.5   1.0 km

Agar Drive, then turn left immediately on a road leading to the Coast Guard Station.

Western Grebes often gather to the west of the breakwater, and **Common** and **Red-throated loons**, **Horned** and **Pied-billed grebes** and various **diving ducks** frequent the area. In some winters, a **Clark's Grebe** may also be present, occasionally with the Westerns, but usually somewhat aloof from them. **Double-crested Cormorants**, **Dunlin** and various **gull species** often loaf on the breakwater. **American** and **Eurasian wigeon** and **American Coots** frequently graze on the grass between the road and the river during high tide, while low-tide river flats attract **Green-winged Teal**, **Killdeer** and various **gull species**.

Written by John and Shirley Dorsey; revised by Rick Toochin and Martin K. McNicholl

19. Lulu Island: Terra Nova Natural Area and Richmond Trails

The City of Richmond encompasses almost 20 islands, the largest by far being Lulu Island. Much of Richmond's industry and almost all of its residential area is concentrated here between the North, Middle and South arms of the Fraser River. During the last ice age, the area was covered by glaciers; when they receded, they left a huge plain that has evolved into the delta of today. Three-quarters of Richmond's 110 sq km (42 sq mi) lies only slightly above sea level. Sloughs criss-cross the agricultural land, creating a haven for many species of waterfowl. The remaining cottonwood and crabapple stands, which once grew all across Lulu Island, provide a refuge for many species of land birds.

The pressures of urban development have resulted in the loss of prime habitat for wildlife, but there are still areas worth exploring. Of particular significance are the Terra Nova lands in the northwest corner where, in 1996, the voters of Richmond directed city council to preserve 26.7 ha (66 a) of land as a park. Richmond council also set aside 13.7 ha (34 a) of old field habitat, which has subsequently been enhanced with the construction of ponds and a drainage system. Known as the Terra Nova Natural Area, funding for its development came in the form of compensation for habitat lost due to the expansion of Vancouver International Airport.

In addition to Terra Nova, the development of recreational facilities has provided an extensive network of trails, a boon for the birder who enjoys walking or cycling. The North, Middle and South arms of the Fraser River all have extensive dyke sections worth exploring. While walking along the dykes, watch for harbour seals disguising themselves as chunks of floating debris; in April and May sea lions may also be present.

Sturgeon Bank, running the length of the west side of Lulu Island, provides year-round marsh habitat for ducks and migrating shorebirds. Inland, the Shell Road Trail runs through fields of blueberries that thrive on the peat bog; small stands of spruce, cedar, cottonwood and willow abound.

Terra Nova Natural Area
Directions

From Vancouver, Oak Street and the Oak Street Bridge lead south to Highway 99, which bisects Lulu Island, and this is the best access route. Exit at No. 4 Road (exit #39B) and continue south for 2 km (1.2 mi), then turn right (west) onto Westminster Highway. The approach to the Terra Nova Natural Area is from Westminster Highway, 4.8 km (3 mi) west of No. 4 Road. Drive west on Westminster Highway, crossing No. 3 and No. 2 roads, to the junction with No. 1 Road. Continue across No. 1 Road and after .4 km (.2 mi), turn right at the stop sign onto Barnard Drive. Continue for .8 km (.5 mi) and turn left onto Westminster Highway again (it is now a small residential street). In .2 km (.1 mi) you will come to the Terra Nova parking area on the left.

Bird Species

Residential development has taken over much of the best agricultural soil in the Lower Mainland. However, the Terra Nova Natural Area allows you to appreciate the land as it used to be. A gravel trail from the parking lot encircles three sides of the Terra Nova Natural Area and links to the West Dyke Trail to complete the west side of the loop; allow at least one hour to walk this.

The first formal bird survey of the new Terra Nova Natural Area was organized by the Vancouver Natural History Society's Birding Section in December 1998, and there have been surveys every month since then. To date, 98 species have been recorded, including some notable sightings of an **American Bittern**, **Ring-necked Ducks**, a **Northern Goshawk**, **Virginia Rail** and **Sora**. With only a few

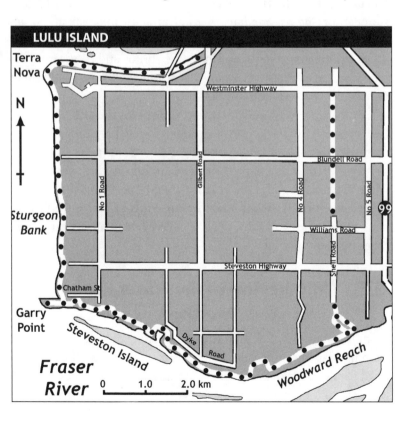

years' worth of information, it is difficult to identify trends. However, the obvious is being confirmed. The area is an important wintering ground for **Mallards** and **American Wigeon**; it supports significant populations of **Great Blue Herons** in the early part of the year; and it provides breeding habitat for good numbers of **Marsh Wrens** and **Savannah Sparrows**. Viewing of shorebirds and water-fowl is best from the platform in the southwest corner of the site, and a spotting scope is recommended here.

Sparrows and *finches* are abundant along the side of the trail wherever there is tangled undergrowth. **Ring-necked Pheasants** thrive in the fields, while **Red-tailed Hawks**, **Northern Harriers** and **Short-eared Owls** can be seen almost all year. These are joined in winter by **Rough-legged** and **Sharp-shinned hawks**, **Peregrine Falcons** and **Northern Shrikes**. Check ditches in late spring and summer for **Spotted Sandpipers**, **Killdeer** and **Cinnamon** and **Blue-winged teal**. During migration periods, *yellowlegs*, *dowitchers* and other sandpipers are present. Check the shrubs and trees across the road from the parking lot towards the north—you may find **Evening Grosbeaks** perched on those branches.

In the northwest and southwest corners of the site, the gravel trail connects to the West Dyke Trail, which provides a view of Sturgeon Bank. In fall and spring the calls of **Snow Geese** fill the air as they gather for migration. **Northern Pintails** live here year round, while **Trumpeter** and a few **Tundra swans** spend the winter here. **American Bitterns**, **Soras** and **Virginia Rails** are secretive inhabitants in this area, and **Barn Owls** and **Peregrine Falcons** can sometimes be seen hunting.

Middle Arm of the Fraser River
Directions

From the Terra Nova Natural Area it is a short distance to the dyke running east-west along the Middle Arm of the Fraser River. River Road parallels this dyke. From the parking area, exit to the right and turn left onto Barnard Drive at the stop sign. Follow Barnard Drive for .5 km (.3 mi) to the T-junction with River Road. Turn left and continue for .8 km (.5 mi) to the end of the road and the start of the West Dyke Trail. There are several small parking areas here that provide excellent views across the Fraser River and Sturgeon Bank. Washrooms are also located here. The West Dyke Trail can be followed all the way south to Steveston if you feel like a good walk of 5.5 km (3.4 mi) one way or have brought your bicycle. Cycling is a very attractive option in this city surrounded by dykes.

From the West Dyke parking area, drive east on River Road. This will eventually lead you to the No. 2 Road Bridge, but several stops along the way are probably warranted. There are several platform viewing areas including one at 1.7 km (1 mi), near the corner of Lynas Lane, that has a short pier. Good views of the river are possible here, but you can walk onto the dyke at almost any point and scan the river. At 2.2 km (1.4 mi) a turn to the right allows you access back to No. 2 Road, but heading south only!

Bird Species

The parking areas at the west end of River Road mark the beginning of the Sturgeon Bank marshes. The West Dyke Trail starts here and runs south to Steveston's Garry Point Park. *Canvasbacks*, *Northern Shovelers* and *American Coots* are often seen from the dyke, and *Red-throated Loons* frequent the river in winter. *Bald Eagles* have nested in trees midway between the two parking areas. Uncommon visitors to the area, such as *Cattle Egrets* and *Long-eared Owls*, have been seen in the marsh and ditches from this trail.

Great Blue Herons are common along the length of the dyke along the Fraser River, and *Canada Geese* can be seen at most times. Scan flocks in autumn and winter for *Greater White-fronted Geese*. From October to April there are large numbers of *Mallards* and *American Wigeon*. Watch for *Gadwall*, *Green-winged Teal* and *Greater* and *Lesser scaup* among them. Check the wigeon closely, because there are often several *Eurasians* to be found. Common sightings farther out on the water are *Double-crested* and *Pelagic cormorants*, *Red-breasted Mergansers*, *Surf Scoters*, *Buffleheads*, *Common Goldeneyes*, *Ruddy Ducks*, *Red-throated* and *Common loons*, plus *Western* and *Red-necked grebes*. Less often seen in the river are *Long-tailed Ducks*, *Barrow's Goldeneyes* and *Common Mergansers*. *Pied-billed* and *Horned grebes* are common close to shore and *Eared Grebes* have been seen occasionally. Look for *Common Snipe* and *Red-winged Blackbirds* in marshy areas.

Steveston and Southern Lulu Island Dykes and Trails

The historic community of Steveston, in the southwest corner of Richmond, provides the visitor with many other attractions in addition to its wildlife. Several eco-tour companies offering boat trips have their base here, and there are historic buildings to visit, as well as a variety of shops and restaurants. The West Dyke Trail ends here at Garry Point Park, but the dyke walk continues eastwards as the South Dyke Trail and Dyke Road.

Directions

To reach Steveston by car, drive south from Westminster Highway on No. 1 Road for 4.8 km (3 mi), crossing Steveston Highway and turning left (west) onto Chatham Street. Continue for a few blocks to reach Garry Point Park and the south end of the West Dyke Trail.

Dyke Road, which runs roughly east-west along the south side of Lulu Island, can be reached by following the South Dyke Trail east from Steveston or by driving south from Westminster Highway on Gilbert Road for 5.8 km (3.6 mi). Gilbert Road runs in a north-south direction between No. 2 and No. 3 roads. Dyke Road and the trail continue east along the South Arm of the Fraser River for another 1.2 km (.7 mi) to a parking area at the south end of No. 3 Road.

22. Bonaparte's Gull

23. Long-tailed Duck
(winter male)

24. Rough-legged Hawk

25. Short-eared Owl

26. Bushtit

27. Mountain Bluebird
(male) (Below right)

28. Green Heron at Jericho ponds

29. Wood Duck (male)

30. Barrow's Goldeneyes, Greater Scaup and Surf Scoters off Stanley Park seawall

31. Sanderling at Boundary Bay

32. Pileated Woodpecker and nestlings

33. White-tailed Ptarmigan

Bird Species

Follow the South Dyke Trail east and watch for a variety of birds on the river. **Green Herons** can sometimes be found in the sloughs. **Barn**, **Tree** and **Violet-green swallows** are common throughout the summer, and **Northern Shrikes** frequent the area in winter. **Savannah Sparrows** can be found here for most of the year; in summer they are abundant, and one or two **Lincoln's Sparrows** can often be found with them in spring and fall. Gilbert Beach, at the south end of Gilbert Road, is a good area to check for **ducks** and migrating **shorebirds**, including **Whimbrel**.

Garry Point Park, the Steveston waterfront and Dyke Road along the South Arm of the Fraser River are probably the best spots for gull watching. Look for **Thayer's**, **Herring**, **Glaucous-winged**, **Mew**, **Ring-billed** and **Bonaparte's gulls**. **Brewer's Blackbirds** and **Brown-headed Cowbirds** can be found most of the year in Garry Point Park along with **Northwestern Crows** and the occasional **Common Raven** in winter.

Shell Road Trail
Directions

Shell Road Trail runs north-south alongside a railway line for 6.5 km (4 mi) and provides some of the best habitat for passerines on Lulu Island. While the whole trail is worth exploring, the southern end and the section between Westminster Highway and Blundell Road provide the best birding. Intermediate points on the trail can be reached where it intersects Westminster Highway, Granville Avenue, Blundell Road, Williams Road or Steveston Highway: each crosses the trail 5.6 km (3.5 mi) east of No. 1 Road.

Bird Species

The hedgerows along the trail provide a year-round home for **Spotted Towhees**, **Bewick's** and **Winter wrens**, **American Robins**, **Bushtits**, **Black-capped Chickadees**, **House** and, sometimes, **Purple** *finches*, **Pine Siskins** and **American Goldfinches**. The fall migration brings **Yellow-rumped Warblers**, **Western Tanagers**, **Red Crossbills** and birds that winter here, such as **Downy Woodpeckers**, **Northern Flickers**, **Varied Thrushes**, **Dark-eyed Juncos**, **Golden-crowned** and **Ruby-crowned kinglets**, and **White-crowned** and **Golden-crowned sparrows**. Spring brings the migrant breeding birds, such as **Rufous Hummingbirds**, **Wilson's**, **Townsend's**, **Orange-crowned** and **MacGillivray's warblers**, **Black-headed Grosbeaks** and **Swainson's Thrushes**. **Hermit Thrushes** are common migrants. Between Francis and Blundell roads listen for the songs of **Willow Flycatchers**; each spring these birds return to breed and can be heard on almost any summer day.

Written and revised by Eric Greenwood

Vancouver Natural History Society
P.O. Box 3021, Vancouver, B.C. V6B 3X5
Events and Information, and **Bird Alert**
Tel: (604) 737-3074, 24 hours a day

20. Burns Bog Area

In satellite photographs of the Lower Mainland, Iona Island is a tiny speck and Reifel Migratory Bird Sanctuary is barely discernible. By contrast, Burns Bog stands out as the largest green space in Greater Vancouver. It is, in fact, the largest urban green space and the largest raised peat bog in all of North America.

The following description includes not only the bog itself, but also the surrounding flood plain, forests and urban ravines that have helped create the bog we see today. On a single hike through this region you can sample almost all of the local habitats, from riparian forest and towering conifers to pine meadows. It is a little like hiking up one of the local mountains, with a fraction of the effort.

The first humans to use the bog were First Nations peoples, including the Katzie, who believed **Sandhill Cranes** were the guardians of the bog. In 1882, the Marquis of Lorne purchased Burns Bog from the surveyors for $1.00 per acre, under an agreement to reclaim the land. In 1905, Dominic Burns bought the bog, and later sold it for peat farming. Since the peat-harvesting operations stopped (a remnant of this industry can still be seen in the large factory at the corner of 72nd Avenue and Highway 91), there have been many applications to develop the bog. The Municipality of Delta has refused each proposal, under pressure from such groups as the Burns Bog Conservation Society and the Vancouver Natural History Society.

The bog itself can be divided into four regions. The sphagnum heathland is characterized by Labrador tea and velvet blueberries, and appears more like Arctic and alpine taiga than the surrounding habitats. Many ponds have formed where peat-cutting operations occurred in the past. Pine/heath woodlands surround the heathland. Here, shore pine and salal predominate. Finally, the outskirts of the bog are composed of two regions—mixed forests and coniferous forests.

Burns Bog contains many endangered and unusual species of plants, animals and insects. Black bears still inhabit the bog, as do fairly large groups of black-tailed deer and the endangered southern red-backed vole. Over 4,000 species of invertebrates have been estimated to occur in Burns Bog. Probably of most interest to birders are the butterflies and dragonflies. Forty-six species of moths and butterflies have been identified in the bog, including the mariposa copper and pine elfin. Burns Bog is one of the best places in the Lower Mainland to find dragonflies, with 25 species documented so far, including the crimson-ringed whiteface, yellow-legged meadowhawk, chalk-fronted corporal, zigzag darner and subarctic darner. Most of these species can be hard to find elsewhere in the Vancouver area. The incredible diversity of plant and animal life in Burns Bog makes the preservation of this unique and special place extremely important.

Note: Travel in the bog is often treacherous and always wet, so rubber boots are a must. Expect to take longer than usual to cover distances. Burns Bog itself is off limits to the public and is extremely hazardous. Peat excavation in the past has created deep ponds and water-filled ditches, many of which are concealed by vegetation. Stay on the trails described below unless you are on an organized tour.

Burns Bog
Directions

There are only two legal public entrances to the bog, since two-thirds of it is privately owned, and trespassing is discouraged. The 72nd Street entrance can be reached by taking Highway 99 south from Vancouver and turning west (right) on Highway 10 (exit #20) towards Ladner, then north (right) onto 72nd Street. The bog is accessible only via a small tunnel under Highway 99. (This tunnel is closed from 6 to 9 A.M. and 3 to 6 P.M. on weekdays.) Alternatively, Burns Bog can be reached at any time from the northbound lanes of Highway 99 by taking the River Road exit (#28) just south of the George Massey Tunnel. Taking the first right (60th Avenue) and then turning right again onto 64th Street will lead you to 72nd Street. There is parking along 72nd Street, before you reach the No Parking signs.

The other entrance is through the Delta Nature Reserve. The entrance recommended by the Burns Bog Conservation Society is from Highway 91 south. Take the River Road exit shortly after crossing the Alex Fraser Bridge. Turn right at the second set of lights (Nordel Court) and follow this road into the parking lot of the Great Pacific Forum (a recreation complex) at 10388 Nordel Court. Park at the back of the parking lot and walk in to the Delta Nature Reserve, following signs that welcome you to the reserve. In approximately five minutes, you will come to a two-headed wooden carving at the beginning of the path that loops through the reserve. Sections of boardwalk are being installed as funds are raised, but rubber boots will still be necessary at almost any time of year.

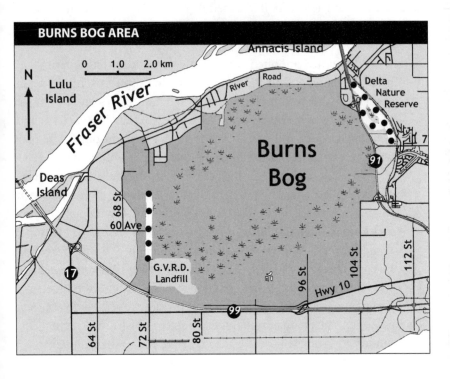

Because of the fragile state of the habitat, dangerous ditches and ponds, and problems surrounding the legality of access to the bog itself, visitors who are unfamiliar with Burns Bog are encouraged to participate in a guided tour run by the Burns Bog Conservation Society (see page 226). Knowledgeable guides offer tours of both the Delta Nature Reserve and the main bog, owned by the Municipality of Delta.

Bird Species

Despite the ecological variety offered by the bog, few people have birded in the area. Just over 150 species have been reported so far from the bog (about 200 species when including surrounding areas). With such a short history of exploration by birders, there is a very real possibility of discovering something new. Part of the difficulty of birding in the bog is that it is mostly privately owned and hard to gain access to. It is hoped that this will change, as it becomes increasingly likely that the bog will be bought and preserved as a park.

While birds are often surprisingly difficult to find, the uniqueness of this habitat in the Lower Mainland attracts some different species to the region. It is one of the few places in the Lower Mainland where **Dark-eyed Juncos**, **Northern Harriers** and **Sandhill Cranes** still nest at sea level. Birders can only anticipate what new surprises lurk in less-explored regions of the bog.

The wide bark-mulch trail at the foot of 72nd Street provides a good walk along a hydro right-of-way. **Raptors** can often be seen soaring overhead. The mixed forest to the left may contain **Anna's** and **Rufous hummingbirds**, **Ruffed Grouse**, **Barred Owls**, **Western Wood-Pewees**, **Willow Flycatchers**, **Common Ravens**, **Warbling Vireos**, **Orange-crowned**, **MacGillivray's** and **Wilson's warblers** and **American Goldfinches**. The forest edges around the blueberry farm to the left of the trail (the farm is private property—do not trespass) can shelter many migrants in spring. Listening carefully for sounds and songs of these birds will alert you to their presence.

The bog habitat to the right (east) is covered for miles with small stunted trees and seems completely devoid of birds except for **Common Yellowthroats** and **Dark-eyed Juncos** (which nest in the bog), and occasional **Orange-crowned** or **Yellow-rumped warblers**.

Raptor surveys have indicated that concentrations within the bog may be even higher than in the surrounding farmland, which has the highest known density of wintering raptors in Canada. **Rough-legged** and **Red-tailed hawks** winter in the pine/heath woodlands, while **Northern Harriers** are year-round residents in both the heathlands and pine/heath woodlands. **Peregrine Falcons** occasionally visit the lagoons, and **American Kestrels** can sometimes be found in the open heathlands in winter. **Short-eared Owls** hunt at dusk and dawn.

In the bog itself, there are several small rush-fringed ponds and lagoons that were created by peat-cutting operations 50 to 60 years ago. These ponds attract many species of water birds. Likely breeders include **Pied-billed Grebes**, **Mallards**, **Gadwall**, **Green-winged**, **Blue-winged** and **Cinnamon teal**, **Northern Shovelers**, **American Wigeon** (uncommon) and **Ring-necked Ducks** (uncommon). This is the only location in the Vancouver Checklist Area where **Ring-necked Ducks** are known to breed. These ponds are also one of the area's major breeding locations for **American Bitterns**. **Soras** and possibly **Virginia Rails** also breed here, and **American Coots** are winter residents. Various species of shorebirds pass through on migration, including **Least**, **Pectoral** and **Baird's sandpipers**, while others, such as **Spotted Sandpipers**, **Killdeer** and **Common Snipe**, stay to breed.

Burns Bog is one of two locations in the Vancouver Checklist Area (the other being the Pitt Wildlife Management Area) where **Sandhill Cranes** are known to nest. Recent reports suggest that about 10 birds may be in the bog during breeding season. Another 10, possibly from the Pitt WMA, join them in September. More pass through briefly during migration. All leave, along with most other water birds, during the fall hunting season. The cranes are seen most easily in the lagoons and surrounding heathland. Since this species is threatened throughout B.C., and particularly in the Lower Mainland, birders should be very careful not to disturb the birds, which may be nesting nearby. Outside the bog, good viewing locations are the fields and ditches along 96th and 104th streets, as well as Crescent Slough near 60th Avenue.

The Delta Nature Reserve portion of the bog is much less wild. The trail is gravel with sections of boardwalk, and it is popular among dog walkers and cyclists. **American Dippers** have been seen feeding in the small pond at the foot of Blake Drive, as well as in the first kilometre (.6 mi) of Cougar Creek. The ravine at the foot of Blake Drive can be quite rewarding for **songbirds**, and sometimes **Barred Owls** can be found there.

The bog vegetation in this area is primarily deciduous and harbours many songbird species in summer, such as **Hutton's, Cassin's, Red-eyed** and **Warbling vireos, Black-throated Gray, Yellow** and **Orange-crowned warblers, Black-headed Grosbeaks** and **Bullock's Orioles**. The wetlands around Cougar Creek (the small stream next to the trail) can produce **Green Herons, Virginia Rails** and **Soras** in summer. It is one of the last remaining strongholds of **Ruffed Grouse** in the Vancouver Checklist Area. Wintering species include **Fox Sparrows** and **Spotted Towhees**.

After about 1 km (.6 mi), a trail leads off to the left (west) through a dense young coniferous forest with nesting **Brown Creepers, Pacific-slope Flycatchers** and **Townsend's Warblers**. After a very short distance, the forest opens up into heathland similar to the habitat described above, before looping back to the main trail. The loop is 2 to 3 km (1.2 to 1.9 mi) in length.

Gull-Watching Areas

The City of Vancouver landfill at the north end of 72nd Street in Delta (see "Directions," above) is home to the largest winter congregation of gulls in British Columbia; tens of thousands feed there during dumping periods (most weekdays from daybreak until 4 P.M.). Although the landfill itself is *strictly out-of-bounds to birders,* most of the gulls spend a significant amount of time lounging around the fields surrounding Burns Bog, particularly during wet weather—a common occurrence during Vancouver winters!

Directions

The best fields are found to the south of the bog along Burns Drive, which can be reached by exiting from Highway 99 onto Highway 10 at the Mathews exchange (exit #20). Turn left at the traffic lights onto Highway 10, and follow the overpass to the second set of traffic lights. Turn left here onto Burns Drive, which runs parallel to Highway 99. Good locations to the north of the bog include the log booms in the Fraser River along River Road, the fields along River Road (especially those around 68th Street) and the fields at 68th Street and 60th Avenue.

Note: In this area, streets run north-south and avenues run east-west; both are numbered. Consult your map for clarity.

Bird Species

Burns Drive provides viewpoints over several very large cultivated fields that attract large flocks of roosting gulls in winter. Gulls to be expected here, in decreasing order from abundant to very rare, are: *Glaucous-winged*, *Thayer's*, *Ring-billed*, *Mew*, *Herring*, *California*, *Western* and *Glaucous gulls*. Glaucous Gulls, the rarest of this group, are more often sighted in the fields to the north of the bog and in the Fraser River. One or two *Slaty-backed Gulls* have been seen consistently for several years, mostly in the fields along Burns Drive. *Iceland Gulls* and *Common Black-headed Gulls* have also been reported occasionally among gull flocks.

For more gull-watching locations, see the 72nd Street information in the "Boundary Bay—64th Street to 112th Street" section.

In addition, the landfill supports the largest number of wintering eagles in the Vancouver Checklist Area. Over 200 *Bald Eagles* have been counted at one time. Over 100 of these birds roost on private property near Deas Island, and can be seen by turning left (north) off River Road onto Vasey Road (turning right here leads onto 60th Avenue) and viewing them from the dyke. (Consult your map for clarity.) Other raptors, such as **Red-tailed Hawks** and **Northern Harriers**, also visit the area. Keep a lookout for the tame Harris's Hawk, which a falconer employs to discourage gulls from feeding at the landfill.

The fields to the north of the bog occasionally have foraging **Sandhill Cranes** (especially in Crescent Slough). **Cattle Egrets** are rare to the north of the bog in late fall.

Written by Kyle Elliott

Eurasian and American Wigeon

Vancouver Natural History Society
P.O. Box 3021, Vancouver, B.C. V6B 3X5
Events and Information, and **Bird Alert**
Tel: (604) 737-3074, 24 hours a day

Burnaby

21. Burnaby Lake Regional Park

Burnaby Lake Regional Park, situated in the middle of the City of Burnaby's Central Valley, is bounded on the south by Highway 1 (the Trans-Canada Highway) and on the north by a main railway line. The north side of the park and its eastern and western ends all offer excellent birding; on the south-side trails, although birding can be good, the vehicle noise from the adjacent Trans-Canada Highway can be very intrusive.

The lake and its surrounding forests and wetlands provide year-round birding, but can be particularly worthwhile to visit during spring and fall migrations. At any season, but particularly during migrations, there is always the chance for unusual birds or an occasional rarity to show up. Summer will present the birder with opportunities to observe many of the typical breeding birds of the forested and freshwater habitats of the Lower Mainland. In winter, the park offers good locations to observe a large variety of the birds that winter in the Lower Mainland, move down from higher elevations or are resident year round.

The land occupied by the park was extensively logged around the turn of the last century, and while walking the many forest trails you can still see much evidence of this activity. Large western red-cedar stumps, with the springboard holes still visible, dot the forested areas. Just west of the Nature House at the foot of Piper Avenue, the remnants of a sawmill can be identified by the large mound of sawdust and wood waste now being colonized by birch and western hemlock trees.

The major habitats of the park are the shallow lake itself, the lowland second-growth mixed forest through which most of the trails wind, and the extensive marshy wetlands forming the margins of the lake. The marshes reach their greatest extent at the eastern end where the lake empties into the Brunette River, which then flows east to the Fraser River. Still Creek feeds Burnaby Lake from the west; to the south, flowing into the lake near the Rowing Pavilion, is the outlet stream of Deer Lake, Deer Lake Brook.

Directions

There are many access points to the park, but the three recommended for birders are the Nature House, Avalon Avenue (Cariboo Dam) and the Burnaby Lake Pavilion. All have good parking, but the Nature House parking area often fills up on sunny weekends. Unfortunately, the parking areas are subject to thefts from cars, so please do not leave valuables in your car while birding. It is possible to make a complete circuit of the lake on foot—approximately 9 km (5.6 mi)—via the trail network.

All directions given here are based on driving east from Vancouver on Highway 1.

To get to the Nature House, take the Sprott Street exit (#32). Turn left onto Sprott Street, continue .6 km (.4 mi) to the first set of traffic lights, and turn left onto Kensington Avenue North. Travel north 1 km (.6 mi), following the signs for Lougheed Highway East over the Kensington overpass. Keep to the right on the overpass and, as you come down the off-ramp, turn right immediately at its foot onto Winston Street. Follow Winston Street east for 2.7 km (1.7 mi), watching out for the green and yellow GVRD Parks sign to Burnaby Lake Regional Park on the right. Turn right onto Piper Avenue and continue past Warner Loat Park on your left, proceed over the railway tracks and at the south end of Piper look for a parking spot.

Note: From the Nature House, trails lead east and west along the lakeshore. The trail heading east is recommended for birders and is

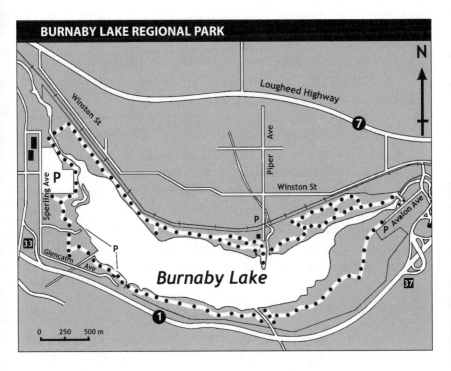

BURNABY LAKE REGIONAL PARK

Lougheed Highway

Winston St

Piper Ave

Winston St

Sperling Ave

P

Glencairn Ave

P

Avalon Ave

P

Burnaby Lake

0   250   500 m

described in the text below. However, the trail heading west is also good, particularly if you continue about 1.5 km (.9 mi) to the turn north to Still Creek. The section of trail from here to the creek bridge can be very productive.

To get to the Avalon Avenue (Cariboo Dam) area, take the Gaglardi Way exit (#37). Turn right at the first set of traffic lights and almost immediately turn left at the next set of traffic lights onto Cariboo Road North. As you come under the overpass, watch for Avalon Avenue almost immediately on your left. Turn left and continue on Avalon, past the sign that indicates Burnaby Lake Regional Park (Cariboo Dam), to the parking area on the right at the end of this short road.

To get to the Burnaby Lake Pavilion, take the Sprott Street exit (#32). Turn left onto Sprott Street, continue to the first set of traffic lights and go straight through, crossing Kensington Avenue North. Drive past the tennis courts on your right to the T-junction and turn right onto Sperling Avenue. Drive past the rugby fields on the left, and turn left following the sign to the Canada Games Rowing Course, Burnaby Lake Pavilion. After a short distance you will arrive at a parking area. (The left turn off Sperling is Roberts Street, but at the time of writing it was not signposted.)

The observation deck of the pavilion provides an elevated view over the lake. From late summer through winter and spring, it is a good place to observe waterfowl and shorebirds. The latter are frequently visible feeding along the far shore of the lake.

The trail that leaves the pavilion parking lot at its southwest corner is recommended. It heads south and then turns east to skirt the lake after crossing Deer Lake Brook. After the bridge, the trail goes through a productive riparian area for the next 200 to 300 m (650 to 1,000 ft) and gives good views of the lake.

Bird Species

Start at the Nature House at the foot of Piper Avenue. A short walk south of the Nature House brings you to Piper Spit, which is bordered on its eastern side by a large mud flat created by Eagle Creek. This is one of the best places in the park to observe shorebirds. In spring and fall migrations, **Long-billed** and **Short-billed dowitchers** and **Western**, **Least**, and **Pectoral sandpipers** frequent the mud flats. Even in winter **Greater Yellowlegs** may be found here along with **Dunlin**. Walk out on the spit for good views of the lake, a prime location for **Wood Ducks**; Burnaby Lake holds the largest population in the Vancouver area. **Mallards**, **Common Mergansers**, **Buffleheads** and **Green-winged Teal** are among the common ducks of winter. Also seen are **Northern Pintails**, **Northern Shovelers**, **Gadwall**, **American Wigeon**, **Canvasbacks**, **Greater** and **Lesser scaup**, and **Common Goldeneyes**. Occasionally, **Blue-winged** and **Cinnamon teal** are seen in spring and summer. **Bald Eagles** nest near the lake, and a couple of nests can be seen by looking south across the lake from the spit. The spit provides excellent viewing up and down the lake and over the surrounding marshes, where, in spring and summer, **Red-winged Blackbirds**, **Common Yellow-throats** and **Marsh Wrens** are common. Many **Great Blue Herons** stalk the lakeshore and marshes here year round. **Double-crested Cormorants** are common in winter. **Northern Harriers** and, less commonly, **Short-eared Owls** hunt over these marshes. In fall, look for the rare **Green Herons** and in winter, **Northern Shrikes**.

Take the trail that heads east across Eagle Creek and is signposted to the Cariboo Dam. This trail passes through an attractive sample of the mixed forest that is very typical of the area and contains the birds you would expect to see in this habitat. In the forest, look for **Black-capped** and **Chestnut-backed chickadees**. In the cooler months, they are often found in mixed flocks with **Golden-crowned** and **Ruby-crowned kinglets**, **Red-breasted Nuthatches** and the occasional **Brown Creeper**. Also look for **Downy Woodpeckers** and the less common **Hairy Woodpeckers**. A cold winter with heavy snows in the North Shore mountains often results in numbers of **Red-breasted Sapsuckers** in this forested area. In the understory, **Winter** and **Bewick's wrens**, **Song Sparrows**, **Dark-eyed Juncos** and **Spotted Towhees** are common. At all times raucous **Steller's Jays** are a noisy presence in the forest, as are **Northwestern Crows** and, less frequently, **Common Ravens**. In fall, winter and early spring these forested areas often have flocks of **Pine Siskins**, **Evening Grosbeaks** and **Red Crossbills** feeding in the upper canopy of the forest. In the spring the forests attract good numbers of **Yellow-rumped Warblers**. **Black-throated Gray Warblers** and **Wilson's Warblers** are also fairly common and breed here. At a number of points the trail comes close to the edge of the marshes, where beavers are actively putting their stamp on the local hydrology. In spring, from March on, **Virginia Rails** are quite vocal in these areas.

You can continue to walk along this trail, cross the Brunette River via the Cariboo Dam, and walk around the entire lake. After crossing the Cariboo Dam, the trail soon arrives at the parking area for the Avalon Avenue entrance. The forest surrounding this parking area is probably the most consistent location in the park to see **Pileated Woodpeckers**. The large cottonwoods between the parking area and the Brunette River are usually good in the late spring for **Red-eyed Vireos** and, in migration, **Cassin's** and **Warbling vireos**. **Wood Ducks** nest here in the many nest boxes erected by members of the Burnaby Lake Advisory Committee.

Continuing on the main trail, a large area of hardhack with many equestrian trails through it is an excellent place to observe displaying **Rufous Hummingbirds** in March and April. From the parking area, the section of the main trail that heads south for about 300 m (984 ft) is an excellent place for many **warblers** in spring, including **Yellow** and **Orange-crowned**, in addition to the species mentioned above.

Written and revised by George Clulow

22. Deer Lake Park

Deer Lake Park, like its close neighbour Burnaby Lake, is located in the Central Valley of the City of Burnaby. It lies south of the Trans-Canada Highway and is much quieter and more secluded than its partner park north of the highway. Whereas Burnaby Lake Park is surrounded by industry, railways and highway, quieter suburbs surround Deer Lake. Like Burnaby Lake Park, it was logged around the turn of the last century and its forested areas are now dominated by mixed second-growth forest.

What is now the western part of the park, between Royal Oak Avenue and the lake, was once the farmland for the Oakalla Prison Farm. The prison has been replaced by the condominiums that overlook the park from the south, but the farm fields are one of the most valuable habitats of the park. This old field habitat—fast disappearing throughout Greater Vancouver—is a tremendous asset to the park, adding substantially to its diversity of birds.

34. Long-eared Owl

35. Crested Myna at
2nd and Wylie in
Vancouver
(Below left)

36. Brown Creeper

37. Song Sparrow (gray
Pacific northwest race)

38. Northern Goshawk

39. Virginia Rail

40. Young Short-eared Owls

41. Wood Duck (female) and family at Jericho ponds

42. White-crowned
Sparrow

43. Hairy Woodpecker